The Social Golfer

Ian William Halliwell

The Social Golfer
published on behalf of the author
in the UK in 2008
by
BRIDGE BOOKS
61 Park Avenue
Wrexham
Ll12 7AW

CIP Data for this book is available
from the British Library

ISBN 978-1-84494-049-3

All profits from the sale of this book will go to the Stoke Association

Printed and bound by
CTPS
China

This book is dedicated to:

My wonderful wife, Karen, and my children – Paul, Emma, Shelley and Tanya. They are my reason to live, my inspiration in my most troubled times.

Family and friends too numerous to mention, who have all given Karen so much support in our darkest hours.

Belatedly to Dad, always there. I hope he would be suitably proud.

The staff at the Countess of Chester Hospital Stroke Unit and at Bridgewater Rehabilitation Ward, Leigh Infirmary, true professionals to whom I owe my continued good quality of life.

The Stroke Association who were always on hand with support, advice and assistance for Karen and I when needed.

My fellow social golfers, without whom my golfing journal would not have been possible.

Contents

Preface   7

Acknowledgements   9

Introduction   11

Trips for the Boys (pre-stroke)   13

    1.   Tunisia   15

    2.   Costa del Sol   21

    3.   Tenerife   27

    4.   England and Wales   33

    5.   South Africa   38

Golf and My Stroke   45

    6.   A Bad Stroke   47

    7.   Nailcote – the British Par Three Championship   52

    8.   Carden Park – the MRC Golf Classic   57

Trips with the wife and friends (post-stroke)   59

    9.   Florida   61

    10.   Australia   69

    11.   Hong Kong   98

    12.   South Africa   103

    13.   The Social Golfer   115

    14.   Conclusion   126

    15.   Stroke – Act Fast information   128

Preface

In September 2007, Ian Halliwell organised a Charity Celebrity Golf Day at Carden Park, Cheshire, in aid of the Stroke Association, which subsequently raised over £10,000. The previous day, he had held a champagne reception where the guests-of-honour were the staff of the Stroke Unit at the Countess of Chester Hospital. Over thirty members of staff attended. One member, Emma, from the physiotherapy department, could not attend but sent the following card, which perhaps sums up the determination and effort required by Ian to get back into golfing, and the spirit with which he faced this battle.

> 3rd September 2007
>
> Dear Ian,
>
> Just a note to apologize for not being able to make it to the event this evening – I know I am going to miss out on a fun night! I hope that the golf tournament will be a huge success, I think it such a great way to raise awareness of the purpose of The Stroke Association.
>
> On a personal note I just want to say how much I enjoyed treating you and in particular how inspired I was by the brave and determined way you dealt with your misfortune. It is not often that a patient propels me to endeavour to make changes to my outlook on life so thank you.
>
> Enjoy tonight,
>
> Kind regards
>
> Emma (physio)
> x

Ian Halliwell, Chairman of the Board at leading recruitment provider MRC International, last night organised a private Chairman's Dinner for nurses at the Countess of Chester Hospital and presented a cheque in grateful thanks for the care he received after his stroke less than a year ago.

Staff at MRC International sponsored Ian to take part in the British Par Three Championships on 7 and 8 August 2007, where he was partnered with Bernard Hunt MBE, a former Ryder Cup Captain

Frank Worthington, staff from the Countess of Chester and Bob Champion.

and current Captain of the English PGA.

Chester-based recruitment company, MRC International, has presented a cheque for £10,000 to the Stroke Association.

The funds were raised through a celebrity-packed golf day held earlier this month at the De Vere Carden Park Cheshire course, near Broxton.

The Chairman of the MRC board, Ian Halliwell, 48, suffered a stroke in December when he was at work in the company's Chester office and was in the Countess of Chester Hospital for two months. The father of four is now back at work, but is determined to raise both funds and awareness of stroke.

Celebrities at the golf event included *Coronation Street* actor, Tony Barton, impressionist Les Gibson, Grand National-winning jockey Bob Champion, ex-World darts Champion John Lowe, Robbie Williams' father, Pete Conway, and ski-jumper Eddie 'The Eagle' Edwards, who joined with paying guests to take on the eighteen-hole course as four-person teams. A gala dinner and charity auction rounded off the day. Lots included a signed 1966 England football shirt and an autographed pair of Muhammad Ali's shorts.

Julie Ainscow, Regional Communications Officer for the Stroke Association, said, 'Stroke is the country's third biggest killer and a leading cause of adult disability. Stroke does not discriminate and can happen to anyone, at any age, and at any time. We are so grateful to MRC International for their dedication in raising not just vital funds for the Stroke Association, but also important awareness about stroke, recovery and prevention. With the help of our generous donors, we can continue to help those whose lives have been affected by stroke.'

Chester Evening Leader, 13 September 2007

Ian presents Louise Elliott from the Stroke Association with a cheque.

Acknowledgements

Thanks to MRC staff members, Nicola Loughnane, Dave McKenna and Stephanie Bates for their painstaking research and extreme patience.

Felicity Owen and Bernard Stapleton for translating from Wiganese to English.

James Brown at Travelbag for his help in all travel arrangements (www.travelbag.co.uk).

Bernard Hunt MBE for being the inspiration behind this journal.

Louise at the Stroke Association for her help and support in all my charitable endeavours.

The following books which formed the basis of my desire to play on every continent:

Planet Golf by Darius Glover
A Golfer's View by Brad McManus
Extreme Golf by Duncan Lennard
World Atlas of Golf by Pat Ward Thomas
Insight City Guides (the perfect tool when visiting a new city)

Introduction

Mark Twain famously wrote, 'Golf is a good walk spoiled,' and indeed every golfer will have had a day when one can concur with that thought. When the swing totally disintegrates for no apparent reason, usually just after your best round in years, when your new box of balls begins to disappear at a rate of knots; when the weather is as bad as your game, golf can seem both an aimless and costly pastime. No other sport has such a disparity in talent between the successful practitioner and the social golfer. However, when you are faced with the realistic possibility that you have played your last round, then your worst round is better than no round at all.

When recovering at Chester and still unable to move any part of my left-hand-side, I re-played over and over some of the good times I had had as a social golfer. I went over how I would play courses given the opportunity again and read magazines, with a particular interest in overseas courses which I dreamed of playing.

Of course, I could hear the whispers that my golfing days were over, but the desire to play was to prove paramount in my recovery and was fundamental in what became a burning determination to walk again and control my left arm and hand. When, on 18 April 2007, I played the back nine holes at Standish Court and shot thirty-nine (par thirty-four), I realised I could still participate and enjoy this glorious game as I had done before. Over the next few months however, I had to accept that there was residual damage that would not allow me to propel the ball at the distances I had before, but I was still able to compete under this ludicrously fabulous handicap and Stableford system that rewards the less competent.

I also made a conscious effort to put back something into both the sport I loved and the people who helped my recovery. This started by my work colleagues sponsoring me to play in the British Par Three Championship at the splendid Nailcote Hall course. From this, we organised our own Celeb-Am when over forty celebs joined a hundred golfers at Carden Park in a celebration of golf on behalf of the Stroke Association to raise stroke awareness. We raised in excess of £10,000 and I am pleased to say, this will now be an annual event.

At Nailcote, I really got the bug back for social golf, partnering golf legend Bernard Hunt, appearing on TV and playing in front of galleries. It was not the senior tour I envisaged having the opportunity to play in one day, but it was close enough – during this time, Bernard gave me many sage words of advice about golf which no doubt will be shared in the following chapters, but it was one about life which made the most impression. Bernard said my recovery was like getting out of the Road Hole bunker after being stuck under the face. I had put the ball to within six feet of the flag but unless I holed the putt, the bunker shot was wasted, and my life was like that – how I moved on would make the recovery better.

A few weeks later at the Celeb-Am Classic, I partnered Willie Thorne, snooker star and TV commentator, no stranger to personal problems himself. He took Bernard's comments one step further – playing golf was an experience to savour, cherish and enjoy, for you never know when you may pass this way again.

What is social golf? In the past, it was camaraderie with the boys, a 'piss-up' at the nineteenth hole and playing well in good weather on well-manicured and prepared courses. Now I have a bigger perception. It is golf played in the best places, where my wife and friends feel equally at home away from the golf course. It is on 'pleasing-to-the-eye' courses, where nature and sport combine in harmony. It is where history has been made, and you are walking in the footsteps of heroes. It is where you meet new friends, get a new understanding of life, where the competitive side is the last ingredient and how you perform is frankly irrelevant.

With that in mind, I formulated a plan to play on all five major continents, spreading stroke awareness to all I encountered and showing that there can be a fulfilling life after a major illness, while at the same time enjoying all the best attributes of social golf. A new philosophy but the same game with even more enjoyment.

Trips for the Boys (pre-stroke)

The biggest liar in the world is the golfer who claims that he plays the game for exercise.
Tommy Bolt

Drink, opium, gambling – from the clutches of all these it is possible to escape, but never from golf, never! Has anybody ever seen a man who gave up golf?
Sir Henry Rider Haggard (1856-1925)

Like other forms of compulsive behavior, for true golfaholics even nine holes are more than he should attempt, yet 18 holes are not enough to satisfy their insatiable craving for humiliation and self-abuse.
Mark Oman

It's the overwhelming feeling of wonder and tradition that is there, when you step off the first tee at St. Andrews, or Augusta, or Pebble Beach.
Arnold Palmer

Golf is a game to be enjoyed. On a blue-sky day, replete with puffy white clouds, strolling down a fairway with friends is a little bit of heaven on earth.
Frank Coffey

Golf is like a love affair. If you don't take it too seriously it's no fun. If you do take it seriously, it breaks your heart.
Arnold Daly

1. Tunisia

In 2002 and 2003, I took a party of twenty lads and lassies for a week's golfing in Tunisia. Why Tunisia? Muslim with a small 'm', plenty of bars and nightclubs, a casino and a racetrack, ladies of the night, great weather, magnificent beaches, also French with a small 'f', fine restaurants and food, fantastic hotels and finally good cheap golf on quite reasonable courses. Five rounds of golf, all transfers, flights and all-inclusive five-star hotel for less than 500 nicker. Can't beat it … in February 2008, the same deal was still less than £600.

Why then isn't this country over-run with British golfers? Tunisia has suffered from post 9/11 syndrome even more than Morocco and Turkey. Perhaps the bombings in Djerba did not help. However, I believe the reason is principally that because it is a Mediterranean country that finds it hard to compete with Greece and Spain. It is also so un-English compared with its competitors, although even the most uneducated seem to speak our language. Many families and visitors simply prefer the more Anglophile resorts and bring back negative tales about the country. If you think there are a lot of Germans in the Costas then think again. Tunisia is a major destination for our very cost-conscious, quality- and value-minded European cousins. You will also encounter many French and Swedes. On my trips, I have often noted how very Anglo-minded the English in particular can be while abroad. The search for Boddingtons and Guinness, then the delight in finding the obligatory Irish bar (usually next to the good old-fashioned fish and chip shop!).

However, I have visited many times and quite frankly, I love the place. The Tunisians love children and my kids have had many a great holiday there. The men love blondes and can't take their eyes off them; perhaps that's why the wife likes the place! The first time we visited the chic resort of Port El Kantaoui, we were being hassled by one persistent jewellery salesman and he was making a habit of touching up the missus. I was about to say something when across the square, a local constable appeared and clouted the guy bigtime around the ear with a baton. The policeman apologised profusely for the fellow's inappropriate behaviour and dragged him to the local station, clouting him every second step. I was not necessarily sure if the wife was happy at the intervention or disappointed that after this incident, word obviously got round the marina and no-one

Teeing off at Tabarka.

15

Fifth hole at the Flamingo, Monastir.

paid her any significant attention for the rest of the week.

We stayed on the golf trip at the custom-built resort at Hammamet Yasmine about five miles outside the ancient town of Hammamet. This resort on a magnificent bay, has all been built since 1990. It reminds me a bit of Cancun in Mexico. There is no significant culture or history in the resort, it is all first-class, brand spanking-new from the hotels (all at least four stars, the majority five star). A new casino and a marina with obligatory floating restaurants, manicured gardens, new American-type shopping malls, and a kiddies' fun-fair, an ice rink (that must cost a fortune to run in that heat!), bowling alleys, bars and restaurants and rounded off with four miles of spotless beach on the Med. Three classic golf courses are within four miles. All-in-all, it is a fine holiday destination.

Hotel Africana

We stayed at the five-star all-inclusive Africana hotel, right on the beach with two outdoor pools, an indoor heated pool, five restaurants and three bars. I have since been back with the family, such is the great value of the place. For twenty lads, it was fabulous, the only major complaint being the beer, wine and spirits whilst all free, were mainly Tunisian-made and very little imported alcohol could be found, hence the occasional nightly trip out for the Anglophiles to the Old Town in search of the imported ales.

The hotel also had a spa and sauna which many of the lads would frequent, principally because the German women in particular would sauna naked. One of the group, had a particularly nasty party trick. He would urinate on the coals if he saw someone about to enter and time them to see how long they could take the excruciating pungent aroma in the heat of the sauna. One day, it backfired on him when some of the other lads locked him in after his trick. He was only released some fifty minutes later, his body looking like a lobster but his face as white as a ghost. The indoor pool actually showed the lighter side of Tunisian humour. The poolman was thrown into the pool by one or two of the guys every day, yet never moaned once. When six weeks later, I returned with my wife and family and entered the pool area, Ahmed the poolman, saw me and went and jumped fully-clothed into the pool.

The hotel was also pretty lax on who you brought back to the hotel, which was extremely useful for one or two of the single lads. Clearly a party of lads from Merseyside and Manchester attracted a certain type of woman from the town to the hotel (for activities that would not normally be encouraged in a family establishment). Working on the old adage of what goes on tour stays on tour, precludes me from mentioning names, but one lad had the pleasure of a lady of the night who spent the entire performance talking to her mum in Arabic on her mobile only to every so often turn round in English and mutter, 'You're so goooood!' This same pair of lads misplaced their wallets and at the end of the evening, frog-marched the ladies back into the room to strip search them for their wallets. The said wallets were in the bedroom all the time!

There is a local ten-pin bowling alley in Hammamet, which could not cope with our party. Whilst happy to take our money, they certainly earned it. A couple of lads were more wayward with their bowls than with their drives. Often wrecking the game in the next alley, furthermore there is a permanent reminder of our visit with a dent in the wall where Rob Marshall's bowl smashed into it after he slipped and the bowl careered at right angles across two lanes and disintegrated after smashing into the wall.

Carthageland

In Yasmine, there is a very impressive new development called Carthageland with a small funfair, replica *medina* with curio shops, bars, restaurants and a casino (the second in the resort). If you are into gambling, then the casino on the esplanade seemed to have more high rollers. The lads had plenty of enjoyable evenings at Carthageland, with top-quality food and wine as well as rekindling childhood memories on the waltzer and big dipper. One evening, a party got on the train down to Skanes about forty minutes away and enjoyed a prosperous evening at the racetrack.

Other highlights included a trip on a pirate ship around the bay. Typical fare of cheap plonk and food, walking the plank, etc., but cheap and very enjoyable. Visitors beware if visiting the Old Town. Taxis drop you off at the old *medina* and you are immediately inundated with locals inviting you into the *medina* for free drink and food, which will be cake and tea and a carpet-selling exercise. I was used to it so got out of every taxi and on being approached simply shouted 'Not interested in a fucking carpet.' They got the picture and left us alone. The Old Town does have some very reasonably-priced, exceptional quality restaurants. Fish dishes are usually top notch, but I always liked the camel steaks.

There are many reasonably-priced excursions arranged from the hotel but we did not try them on this lads' trip as we had golfed every day, being that Tunisian prices are so cheap, it did not make sense not to. However, the hotels offered day trips to some of the country's most majestic monuments. The Colisseum at El Jem, more magnificent and in better condition than the one in Rome, and the cave houses of Matmata on the edge of the Sahara (where *Star Wars* was filmed) are particularly recommended. Within easy reach are the resorts of Kantaoui and Monastir, whilst Tunis is less than an hour away with a typically Parisian feel for an African capital city. Hammamet Yasmine is an excellent base to see much of this very special country.

I have played every golf course in Tunisia – I wonder how many people can say that about any country – and for a while I was possibly (or so I felt) the leading expert on golf in Tunisia. In 2002, I produced a golf pamphlet for a tourist company which I attach here as probably a more definitive summary of the golf available in this Mediterranean paradise.

On our tour, we played all three courses around Hammamet; all are within fifteen minutes of the resort. The Citrus Course ran out of all their beer and spirits following our day there. We literally did drink them out of house and home. We travelled to Monastir to play the Flamingo Course, possibly my favourite. Always in outstanding condition, with three or four exceptional holes and some stunning views of the sandflats. The eighteenth is a majestic downhill par five, where on our trip, a lady player won the longest drive (much to the chagrin of the bigger hitters). The fairway eventually

View from the tenth tee at the Flamingo, Monastir.

rises to a four-tier green where it is often required to putt back up the hill to remain on a tier level. When I last played, the pin was on the second tier and my approach had finished on the third tier. My caddy advised that I putt up and away on to the fourth tier to allow the ball to roll gently to the pin. I ignored his advice and four putted. He had a go following his preferred line and left it six inches away for an easy tap in.

To complete our trip, we played at Kantaoui, which has hosted PGA events and is famous for being the place where the longest recorded hole in one was achieved. We concluded by playing the Carthage course in Tunis City. I don't recommend this to any discerning golfer, but if you are visiting the city and want a quick round at a reasonably-priced and equipped course, you could do worse, and it has to be said that the Carthage has a fine club-house and restaurant.

I think, and the consensus from the lads was, that we should just have played around Hammamet twice, despite the quality of Kantaoui and Monastir. The one-hour coach ride was a bit off-putting compared with ten minutes to three equally impressive facilities. I strongly advise visitors to use the local caddies for less than a fiver a day. They impart great course knowledge and you would save that on lost balls. They have a great sense of humour too. In Tunis, on reading a birdie putt for one of the guys, the caddy said, 'break to the left two balls.' The player hit it on the right line but the ball sped ten yards past the pin such was the over hit. The player chastised his caddy, 'You said it would break,' to which the reply was, 'You can't even break wind at that bloody speed.'

When I first visited Tunisia in the late '80s, it was easy to put some of the problems encountered on golf facilities down to it being a fledgling golfing country. It still has no heritage as such, no players, and in truth, the courses probably only measure up to being average to good when compared with the Costas or even Morocco, Turkey or the new facilities in Cyprus. There is no brilliant course, however facilities are good and have improved at the nineteenth hole. Usually you can count on them having good food and always plenty of beer and quality wines and spirits, (unless twenty UK lads have consumed it all!) Practice facilities and coaching have improved immeasurably, however. Speed of play, still a problem, is constantly being worked on. The number of Germans and Swedes in particular on the course, who refuse to use buggies or caddies can still make a round take six hours in some places. The standard of green maintenance has improved considerably. On our visit, no-one complained about the standard of the golf courses. However, still without doubt the main attraction is the cost. A week on the Algarve or Costa Del Sol can now set you back about £1,000 with golf accommodation and flights, and that's before food and entertainment come into play. Tunisia is by comparison a steal. You pay for what you get, but in Tunisia, I would argue you get much better value for money than some of its esteemed competitors.

It is also excellent for bringing back duty-free stuff – usually! It did however cause one of my former business associates considerable grief after this lads' tour. One of the guys left his clubs at the hotel, so my friend, Tahar (a well respected and prominent Tunisian businessman), offered to bring them back three weeks later. On arrival at Manchester Airport, he was escorted without reason to the customs interrogating Room. 'Have you anything to declare?' he was asked.

'No,' he replied.

'Do you smoke?'

'No,' he replied honestly.

At which the officer produced and unzipped said golf bag and over 4,000 cigs fell out. My fellow golfer several weeks later did receive his clubs, less the fags and he still now believes Tahar has a *fatwah* on him. Who are we to tell him otherwise!

I also encountered the best of Tunisian hospitality when at Kantaoui golf course I turned my foot over in a pot-hole tearing all my ankle ligaments. After my round (I amazingly shot a sub eighty round on one leg), I was immediately taken to the hospital to be X-rayed and plastered-up. In the theatre, a very large rotund tabby snuggled up next to me when I was X-rayed. So much for Gamma Rays and all that! The hotel ensured I wanted for nothing as I was waited on hand and foot. The local Tunisian Tourist Officer on hearing of my plight ensured I was collected in a limo and taken to the airport. I had my own chauffeur to carry my clubs and case, and Tunis Air flew me home first-class.

Any group of golfers wanting decent golf at very reasonable prices in the sun and exceptional accommodation can do no better than Tunisia, basing themselves at Hammamet Yasmine.

Yasmine Beach – Hammamet Harbour

Tunisian golf offers much variety. In Tabarka, one swings right in the heart of a forest, near duck ponds. In Jerba, one drives a ball within a few feet of sand dunes. Hammamet, Carthage, Kantaoui, Monastir – other Mediterranean landscapes dotted with cypress, orange, olive and palm trees. The golf courses of Tunisia suit all tastes and all levels of challenges, most of them offering wonderful vistas of the sea. The cost of a round is substantially less than that on mainland Europe.

Tabarka Golf Course

Spread over 118 acres in the midst of eucalyptus, pine and oak tree forests, this eighteen-hole, par seventy-two course (now extended to twenty-seven holes) is in perfect harmony with the surrounding verdant countryside. It includes seven holes on the beach and even fords across the sounds. Designed by the architect, Ronald Fream, it is very similar to the Cypress Point Club in California. It is an original course which appeals to the most experienced golfers and is home to the Tunisian Open Challenge.

Golf de Carthage

Located in the heart of a wonderful green area, in the shade of hundred-year-old eucalyptus trees as well as pine, cypress, palm, olive and orange trees, this small eighteen hole golf course (par sixty-six – 4,860 yards) requires skill and accuracy. It is only eight minutes away from the Tunis-Carthage airport and ten minutes from the capital. It has a wonderful club-house and excellent restaurant.

Golf in Hammamet

The Yasmine golf course established in 1990, meanders through the hills between the sea and the forest. Due to its vast driving range and numerous tee-offs per hole, this eighteen hole championship golf course (par seventy-two – 6,726 yards) and nine hole school (par thirty) is suitable for players at all levels and offers a great variety of strokes. It is managed by the Magic Life Group (TO Gulet), the same group that owns the Africana Hotel, and great golf deals are available as well as transport by way of a daily service to and from the course to the hotel.

The Citrus golf, second course in Hammamet is one of the most frequented in Tunisia. Spreading over 173 acres, planted in olive trees and forests, it is made up of two contrasting championship courses (eighteen holes – par seventy-two) 'La Foret' (The Forest) (6,740 yards) and 'Les Oliviers' (The Olive Trees) (6,675 yards) to

Les Oliviers, Hammamet.

Les Oliviers, Hammamet.

which is added a nine hole executive course (par twenty-eight – 1,221 metres). It features the largest driving range in Tunisia, five pitching greens, five putting greens and a capacity of 120 players. It is suitable for all categories of players. Training facilities and coaching here are exceptional.

These two courses have also been designed by Ronald Fream.

El Kantaoui Golf Course

Built in 1979 and extended to 132 hectares, this thirty-six hole (par 144 – 12,536 metres) also designed by Ronald Fream, is a high level course meant for experienced golfers and occupies a prominent place among all Tunisian courses. It consists of two eighteen-hole courses, 'Panorama Course' and 'Sea Course'. In order to better manage the great demand, the course has been equipped with a computerised information service. The course runs along the water's edge and overlooks the charming resort of El Kantaoui.

Monastir Golf Courses

Since August 1994, a second golf course, the 'Palms Links' has been open in Monastir. It is an eighteen hole (par seventy-two – 6,140 metres) championship course located in natural sand dunes and palm trees. It has a nine-hole (par twenty-seven) golf school and a large well-equipped driving range. It is suitable for the average player. Sadly, this does not bear comparison to the courses in Hammamet and the rest of Tunisia. In my opinion, it is the weakest course in the country, although exceptionally well-located to the tourist hotels of Skanes.

The older Monastir golf course 'Flamingo,' (eighteen hole par seventy-two – 6,140 metres) is a highly technical course which spreads from small valleys to water ponds amidst Roman vestiges. Designed by Ronald Fream to answer the needs of the most demanding golfers, it can nevertheless attract all levels of players thanks to its five tee-off areas per hole, and three beginners' holes. This is my favourite and always a pleasure and a test to play.

Djerba Golf Club

Conceived by the British architect, Martin Hawtree, the last-born among the Tunisian golf courses is an eighteen hole par seventy-three – 6,169 metres course with nine executive holes. It spreads over a 120 ha terrain dotted with palm trees, between the sea and the sand dunes. Some fairways are not more than forty-metres wide and end up along the shore. The island of Djerba is truly a paradise and far removed from the African experience of the rest of the country. This sun-soaked corner of Tunisia boasts some of the finest beaches in the Med, arguably the finest. It is much different from the rest of Tunisia in its ethnic mix, with Arabs, Berbers, Jews and Europeans mixing to give a real cosmopolitan feel to the island. In Homer's *The Odyssey*, Djerba is believed to be the fabled legendary land of the lotus-eaters. Most of the hotels in the tourist zone offer exceptional golf deals and all are top-class with spa facilities and restaurants to match the best the rest of the Med can offer.

2. Costa del Sol

The Costa del Sol or Costa del Golf, as the signs continually remind you that this area is self-proclaimed to be, remains the most popular destination for any golf trips from the UK and it's easy to see why. This picturesque part of Andalucia on the Med has a wonderful climate, some exceptional courses, as well as some mediocre ones, it must be said. Several sensational resorts mixed with smaller seaside and mountain villages, more akin to Cornwall than Spain, the area from Malaga down to Gibraltar now hosts over fifty courses and golf is now the principal earner for tourism.

The relative cheapness of flights from both budget and established airlines such as Ryan Air, Easy Jet, Monarch *et al*, has made Malaga accessible at less than two hours from the UK for ludicrously low prices. I have checked this morning and can fly from Manchester to Malaga tomorrow for just £46 return. I cannot travel up to Turnberry or St Andrews for less. Accommodation is also not particularly dear and great deals abound, if you are tasty around the old search engines on the internet. The price of golf since the Millennium however has rocketed in-line with property prices and the extortionate cost of an evening's entertainment in the chic resorts of Puerto Banus and Marbella.

My first visit was in 2001 and having visited on a weekend break in each subsequent year, I have witnessed a major change in the area and in particular the golf experience for visitors. Unless staying in a villa on a specific course, which can be a good option, but limits golfing opportunities elsewhere, nearly all golf visitors base themselves on the golden stretch between Marbella and Estepona, centred around the ludicrously expensive resort of Puerto Banus. I have stayed in two high quality resorts within five miles of Banus at the Golf Caledonia, a fine purpose-built apart-hotel exclusively for golfers, with several bars, indoor and outdoor pools and booking facility for golfers, and the Hotel Paridisius with its own course.

This is a four-star hotel with exceptionally fine facilities, is more family-orientated and again has a golfing co-ordinator to arrange tee times. Whilst both are very comfortable, friendly and ideal places to stay for golfers, the first problem is that they are a taxi ride, (about thirty euros) from the action at Banus. Marbella is even further afield. A car is also essential to get to any golf course, so the costs start to rack up already.

I suppose it's mandatory for any

Slasher, Nik and Russ in Alhaurin.

The boys on cheap beer in Alhaurin.

aspiring social golfer to spend a night in Banus, watching the money go – by standing outside Sinatra's. This is where the golfers all mix, and on my first trip, I stood next to Bill Beaumont and Ian Botham and truly felt I had arrived. At Sinatra's (where it is now at least fifteen euros for a bottle of beer), you can watch the money arrive in the flash Porsches, Ferraris, Mercs and BMWs and see the peroxide women with all the botox and implants. It is really a people-watching paradise. In the last few years, however, there has been a noticeable influx of ladies of the night from eastern Europe, svelte stunners constantly harassing you. Sounds great, but after a while becomes a little irritating. There is not a cheap night to be had in this town because prices of food and drink are outrageous. Entertainment is limited. Joy's Piano Bar remains possibly the focal point of anything remotely interesting. I have seen golfers blow their budget in just one evening here. It is now quite dangerous too, because the Russian Mafia seem to have taken over from the UK East End mob and it can be very daunting and intimidating in certain places and bars. On one visit, the owner of the sex shop in the area was assassinated for not helping a drug dealer hide from the police. Drugs are freely and readily available which is another development over the past three years.

Banus can make sensible individuals behave in totally ludicrous and uncharacteristic ways and can bring out the wannabe in all of us. On my first visit, I went with two friends, one of whom was a retired pro-footballer of some success in the lower leagues, who had for a short period achieved his goal of premiership football at Southampton until injury curtailed his career. Pete felt totally at home in this environment and one evening, we were enjoying a meal at the Greek restaurant on the front just down from Sinatra's. Pete bought a bottle of wine, tasty and exceptional it was. He was about to order another on my round, but the accountant in me came to the fore and I asked for the wine menu to check the cost. Now this was in the days of the *peseta* and after a few beers, my mental maths was causing me a few difficulties but unless I had put the decimal point in the wrong place, that bottle had cost £140. I borrowed a pen and worked it out long-hand on a napkin, yes, £142.56. I informed Pete, who for a minute looked gobsmacked before he regained his composure, 'And worth every penny,' he exclaimed and promptly ordered another.

Thankfully, Mike quickly expressed his view that he would like a Mateus Rose at about a tenner so I was saved from purchasing the most expensive round in my life. We were playing at Club Marbella on 11 September and had just completed our round at 2 p.m.

Entertainment Alhaurin style.

when the planes started to crash into the towers. As usual on completion of a round, Mike and I headed straight to the bar whilst Pete went for a shower. Mike and I were transfixed watching events unfold. When Pete joined us and said after watching a few minutes of the news report, that he had seen this film a few weeks earlier on TV, he felt a bit of a berk when he finally realised what was happening.

A few trips later, in Joy's with a group of eight lads, the attention of three of them was taken by a bunch of Latvian beauties. Terry the elder of the group approached the girls and several minutes later returned informing his mates he had negotiated an hour for just 300 euros for them all, i.e. 100 each and off they went. About ten minutes later, they returned urging us all to head to Marbella. They had entered a local house, had been greeted by the madam and then informed that it was 500 euros each. They had been threatened for wasting the girls' time and charged 100 euros each for the pleasure of walking them to the house and warned in no uncertain terms to get out of town.

More recently, we have stayed in Marbella at one or two of the more reasonable budget hotels, particularly around the pedestrianised Casco Abtigu and Almeda areas. The nightlife is quite good and cheaper food can be found as well as reasonably priced beer. However, it may not be lively enough for some. Indeed, most of my younger, and all of my single friends, always prefer Banus.

Even at Marbella, costs can escalate. Car hire is essential and hotels are pricier than at the tourist resorts of Torremolinos and Fuengirola. These towns probably offer better alternatives for groups wanting continual lively nightlife, certainly in summer, although from October to May only Marbella and Banus offer a busy-enough community to make the evenings buzz.

In recent years, the older, more mature members of our golfing fraternity were sick of the cost of these trips to the sun where the golf was getting dearer and an evening out would cost as much as one hundred quid regularly. We looked at alternatives and found one in the fine old hill-town of Alhaurin El Grande about twenty kms from Malaga on the road to Coin. This pleasant town has many bars including two or three British and Irish ones with a small but vibrant ex-pat community. An Indian, Chinese and several outstanding local restaurants all within walking of the two apart-hotels, both with ideal basic facilities for a group of lads at a cost of less than 100 euros for a long weekend. In Alhaurin, a bottle of beer would cost two euros. So clearly an evening here would never break the bank. This town was ideal for us and we have had three great breaks. Just five kms from the superb Lauro and Alhaurin course, one can enjoy a very cheap weekend's golf at budget prices. Clearly, the quietness of the town would not suit all but it remains my preferred choice, if I choose to visit the Costas again. The town is not always that quiet. On one visit, the chef at the London Bar, a tavern on the square and a very popular and much-frequented establishment, raped and butchered two local girls. It was not an ideal time to have a break, but I have returned since. The guy got life and normal service has resumed.

Alhaurin el Grande: the boys in El Grande

Another alternative away from the golden stretch is to consider a stop in Gibraltar. This wonderful bit of England-in-the-sun is ideally located for the best courses on the Costa, such as San Roque, Sotogrande and Valderrama, which are all closer to Gibraltar than Marbella. Gibraltar offers the best of the UK but in the sun. The 'Cradle of History' as it calls itself, is a fine place to visit on its own; the apes, the tunnels, the battlements are all worth a trip. It is of course a duty-free paradise as well, so I am surprised more golfers do not take advantage of the location. I am particularly fond of Gibraltar, after a round of golf, sitting in MacIntosh Square, drinking English beer in the sun listening to live music and eating fine food (either tapas or fish and chips). It simply cannot be bettered on the Costa.

Turning to the golf, I would place these into three distinct categories: exceptional, that is Valderrama where the Ryder Cup was held, San Roque where the PGA Tour Schools are held. These courses are more expensive and can only really be fully enjoyed by the more competent low-handicapper. High quality courses, not as expensive, still difficult, with a bit of history and plenty of character and attractive to play.

Alhaurin El Grande.

In my opinion, the best of these are: Santa Clara, in the centre of Marbella next to the hospital; the Flamingos, between Banus and Estepona, home of the PGA Seniors Matchplay; Alhaurin, the Seve-designed course just outside the town; and the Lauro, a fine twenty-seven hole set up which remains my favourite in the whole area. And finally the rest, not necessarily bad courses, most are fine like the Rio Real, Club Marbella and Los Naronjos, but there are a few ordinary courses on this stretch like Mijas, Atayala and Parador. I suppose it's all down to individual preference and usually there is a partic-ular reason I did not rate these courses. At Mijas, there were no carts, so we had to walk and the round took seven hours. At Atalaya, it had rained and the course was not playable but it did not have many redeeming features anyway. At Parador, which is right on the flight path to Malaga, the approaching planes were a constant put off. The drive for the seventh is interesting, being next to a naturist beach. A good excuse to be three off the tee.

I have played Santa Clara several times and always fully enjoyed the experience. Some of the holes are quite exceptional, the views down to Gibraltar are stunning. A superb club-house, it is a wonderful place but has become a bit pricey in line with the much more famous courses further west. We played this in 2001 in the first week it opened; everything was pristine – including the buggies with fridges on the back. The eighteenth hole is virtually surrounded by water with a bricked-in cart path round the rear. I parked up and after holing a birdie putt to win the pesetas, in my excitement, reversed into the wall and trashed the fridge.

Los Flamingos is an extremely hilly course, again-like Santa Clara, it opened in 2001 and one of the newer breed, based on more Americanised course construction as opposed to European feel. Again, a superb location that overlooks the Med, fabulous hotel on site, exceptional club-house facilities but once

again the cost is approaching three figures and has increased year-on-year. Plenty of holes where water is strategically placed to offer a fine consequence for golf play but also makes the place a wonderfully attractive course.

Sadly, on my last visit, extremely slow pace had crept in with five hours for the front nine, something that is simply quite unacceptable. The Lauro complex, based on the road to Alhaurin, was

Holes One and Two, Alhaurin Golf Course.

originally a pleasant parkland eighteen hole course, not partic-ularly difficult, only one or two exceptional holes, greens were often slower than many in the area but always guaranteed a four hour round and I always scored well. A *finca* type club-house with brilliant tapas menu supplemented the occasion. In 2003, a further nine-hole loop on the other side of the road was added. This loop on the side of the hill does have a fair number of quality holes. The first tee, next to a pond, is always full of frogs which you can hear throughout teeing off. Bang your club on the rocks and about fifty or more will jump out. The ninth, all downhill, is particularly impressive. The beauty of this addition, however, is that you can now spend a full day here playing nine in the morning, lunch, then eighteen all at a price that other courses in the area can't match. It's also just ten minutes from Alhaurin, so

certainly for a weekend break where you need to maximise golfing opportunities, it has been very popular on our recent trips. It was here that my mate, Nicky, broke his brand new £450 Ping driver. Every golfer in carts will at some time have unbuckled the belts so that they can watch the rather childish image of your competitor's bag falling off. Nick and I did it to Slasher Ken then drove off rapidly down the hill not realising Slasher had reciprocated, Nick's bag fell off at pace snapping his driver in two. That's what I think happened, but maybe it was that Mr Easy Jet broke it on the way home. I think that's the official story line!

The other course we always play is the Alhaurin. This is where Seve, I think, got his own back on the golfing gods. A course, built on the side of a hill into a valley, is a wonderful natural amphitheatre for golf. That Seve decided to place greens in the most improbable positions on the hill and so many blind tee shots makes this an outstanding, but at the same time exhilarating, challenge. The course can only be walked by the fittest (or by the Germans). It is, however, a deathtrap for carts in wet conditions. On our last visit, we were on the second hole, a par four of about 340 yards, driving blind over a fairway that rises about 100 feet to a rapid drop of more than 100 feet to the green. All four of us drove over the ridge and set off in our carts. Russ and Nick went first and disappeared over the ridge and out of view. Slasher was next, and I heard that sickening sound of metal cracking, followed by screams from the guys. When we arrived at the peak, we could see the cart rolling side-on down the hill with the guys trapped underneath. Fortuitously, its mangled remains stopped halfway and the lads were badly cut when we released them. They were both battered and bruised. Then at the seventh, a ninety degree dog-leg right, a drive of about 250 to the corner of the dog-leg, the fairway then simply runs out to a sheer cliff. The fairway turns sharp right dropping two hundred feet to the green. Slasher and I both hit good drives to the apex. Slasher parked up and hit a seven iron to about five feet from the pin. I went to get my eight but the cart set off downhill, only stopping after it careered through the green cleaning out the pin. We later learned that six carts had been written-off that week.

That round ended up with us having a big argument with our German friends. We had followed this four ball for an hour or so, being constantly held up. They had this annoying knack of waiting for the green to clear before playing, even if they were 300 yards away. Eventually at the twelfth I think, another dog-leg left, they were in the fairway at the apex having all played two. They could not reach the green but refused to play. Slasher said, 'Let's drive, we can't reach them.'

All four of us however hit great drives to the apex just short of our friends. Slash and I arrived first, to be greeted with, 'What is your name! I report you,' this blond stereotypical old German shouted arrogantly.

Mentioning 'Royal And Ancient' and loads of other baloney, I quickly replied 'Mike Mallett, Gathurst Golf Club.' Mike, a good mate, can always be blamed for everything and anything on a golf course. As I

Slasher takes a divot.

spell his name out, Nick and Russ come over the hill in their beat-up buggy looking like two yobs who had been in a recent altercation. Boris takes one look at them, then decides he'd better be off. He picked up his ball and marched off to the next tee. They probably got their own back at the eighteenth. On this hole, we all played good drives and approaches which clearly all hit the green but when we arrived there was not a single ball to be seen, but four smiling assassins were walking up the hill to the clubhouse giggling and cackling away.

Despite the unsuitability for buggies in bad weather, on a nice day this is a quality course with some excellent holes. Greens are obviously full of slopes but have always been true and of a nice speed. The first hole is a great start as a par five meandering away from the clubhouse with the fairway in a valley leading to a raised green. As a first tee shot, it simply invites you to cream the ball. Despite major property work that has been on going, with a significant number of villas being developed, the natural beauty of the place has not been lost. On site is the usual hotel with a horse-riding school for those interested and a superb *à la carte* restaurant.

Every year you visit, especially when you head west to Algeciras and Gibraltar on a stretch of road deemed the most dangerous in Europe, you are continually amazed at the property development with villas and golf courses being thrown up in the most inhospitable of places. Prices here have skyrocketed to quite ridiculous levels. If you bought here in the '80s and avoided any land grab, that amazingly apparent legal loophole where councils can grab your land, you would now be sitting on a fortune. However, now is not a good time to buy. In 2003, I looked at properties before electing to buy in Florida. For £120,000, I bought a four-bedroom villa with pool and spa in Orlando. This would barely buy a studio in Marbella.

Whilst I personally would now never go here for anything longer than a long weekend, possibly travelling on a Thursday, returning on a Monday and would stay at Alhaurin or Gibraltar (dependent on where I wanted to play), I can understand why golfers still flock to the golden stretch for their first taste of overseas golf. My friends have in recent years preferred the Algarve to the Costa. I have yet to sample these delights as these trips have usually coincided with the start of university terms for my kids. Having spoken to Russ, Slasher and Mike, all now prefer the Algarve golfing experience but all concur, it is even more expensive.

The town of Alhaurin.

3. Tenerife

Island of sun, great nightlife, sexy women, nice golf – take twenty lads staying in a luxury villa playing four courses all around the island and you have the perfect boys' trip. What could be better?

A good friend of mine and local Wigan businessman, John Roberts, has a villa on the prestigious Golf de Sur complex, close to Playa de las Americas, the Benidorm of Tenerife. Every year, he invites a group of mature laddies to this sunshine paradise to partake in the JR Classic. This test of golf is not just about ability on the course but the mental and physical fortitude to survive seven days on the piss …

We left the UK in mid October on a typical wet and wild Manchester morning. The more hardened amongst us had already began our pre-trip routine. Bacon barm joey, brown sauce and five pints of Boddingtons, with the subsequent four visits to the loo – I always get the first pint, piss-free. Don't know why.

John had surpassed himself with the golfing arrangements. Round one would be at the Tecina Golf Club on the Isle of Gomera about five miles from Los Cristianos. This would involve a ferry trip and overnight stop at the prestigious Tecina Jardin Resort. The second round two days later, would be at the Ballesteros-designed course on the north Coast at Buena Vista, an unique set-up with sets of six par threes, six par fours and six par fives. One way of ensuring a par of seventy-two! The final round would see us back in the south, at the established Amarilla Course in Playa. The keener golfers would conclude the week at the Golf de Sur in a challenge competition.

John's villa was effectively two semi-detached villas knocked through to form one mega villa which

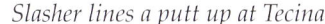
Slasher lines a putt up at Tecina.

Ian on Fourth Tee at Tecina.

could cope with twenty guests. I was in a top-floor twin-bedded room, paired with good mate and established social golfer, Kenny Slasher Jones. Our patio overlooked the seventh hole on the south course of the Golf de Sur, and Kenny and I enjoyed many a San Miguel watching the action and giving appropriate advice to all who would listen as they lined up their putts. The villa was also ideally located for the local cafés for a good old-fashioned English breakfast every morning. Why do we English always have to have our bacon, eggs, sausage, beans, and tomatoes with toast, wherever we are on holiday? We were also only a ten-euro ride and ten minutes from all the action down in the resort.

The first day saw us take the car ferry to Gomera. Now, apparently, there is a passenger ferry straight to the Tecina but we would have had to carry our clubs and bags about 100 yards to the resort as there was no transport. So JR decided to take four cars over, rather than walk these 100 yards! What he didn't tell us was that the trip from the car ferry involved a ten-mile car trip over the mountainous roads, little more than one car width, with drops of over 2,000 feet either side. It was torturous as the brakes stank of burning, as every climb was followed by a descent driven in low gear and continual braking. Unfortunately, JR spent more time looking back and chatting to us than looking forward. I adopted the method by which I go on rides at Disney, I simply closed my eyes until we arrived and tried to ignore the screams from within the car. On arrival at Tecina, twenty ashen-faced golfers leapt from the cars, Kenny kissed the ground and young John went to change his undies. Two cars had clearly severely damaged the brakes, the smell of metal on metal permeated round the car park. It was then I got my first view of the golf course.

The club-house was at the bottom of the hill next to the resort and a fine nineteenth it looked too, but the first hole was apparently two kilometres up the hill on top of the mountain. Stan, John's brother, remarked that at least the course plays the right way – down, not up.

The resort was damn fine

The Fourteenth Green at Tecina.

28

though, the type of place you would like to take your wife or girlfriend to, if not a little quiet for the lads. However, the car journey had taken its toll and most of the lads were very subdued. Even the sight of the usual Germans topless next to the pool did little to raise flagging spirits, either that or everyone was taking this competition a little more seriously than me and Slasher. We had a Stella at the pool bar and remarked at how German women over fifty still managed to get away with thongs at their age. These same women later in the evening would look so prim and proper and so covered-up in styles of clothing long outdated in the UK.

The Eighth at Buena Vista.

The golf next day started in temperatures approaching ninety degrees and unfortunately for all our groups, there were no buggies left. They were all out on the course and would be brought up to us as and when they came in. That was great for the early pairings who got their buggies by the second or third holes, but we were last off and only got ours by the ninth. OK, it was all downhill, but it was unbearably hot and fatigue had already kicked-in. The course itself was, however, very memorable. Some of the views were quite stunning, greens were in excellent condition and, for a course that had to be quite limited in its design as it careered down the hill, had some exceptional holes. In particular the par three, fourth, pictured on the front cover of the book, was simply stunning.

The opening holes are two relatively straight par fours that meander downhill across the hill. Obviously, the fairways are always sloping to the sea, the third, a par five, wanders back to below the first tee, where the early groups collected their buggies and where we realised we were in for a hard first nine. To the turn, the course follows this pattern: left downhill way from the top of the hill, and then a long par five back to the centre. Despite this layout, the course did offer a fair but enjoyable test. The fairways were tight, but well-cut, and drives had to be positioned into the correct area to avoid difficult hanging lies. The greens were all protected by well-maintained bunkers and the greens themselves were full of undulations and quite slick. After the tenth, a driveable slightly uphill par four, the course flattened as we approached the bottom of the hill. A couple of holes were on the coastline giving exceptional views and the usual difficult wind problems. The back nine were heavily wooded as well. I have to say I really enjoyed playing this course, even if my score of twenty-nine points, playing off eleven (John set his own handicaps for all the competitors), was not particularly brilliant. I would recommend any golfer make the effort to get over to La Gomera, which in its own right looks a scenic little beauty of an isle.

That evening back in Playa, we went into the town to sample the nightlife. It was too similar to Benidorm for my liking, lots of English bars with the usual customised British entertainment. Diana Ross

The boys on the Fifth at Amarillo.

and the Supremes look-alikes and the Jackson five at the Motown Bar, The Commitments-replicas at the Irish Tavern with the Wild Rover, whoever he is? Lively it was and ideal for the lads, but not somewhere I would necessarily like for a break with the wife. She says that's the snob in me, perhaps, but I can drive twenty miles to Blackpool for this type of entertainment and nightlife. Next day, we simply relaxed next to the pool and gave plenty of advice to anyone playing the seventh. We then travelled to the north of the island to play Buena Vista. I enjoyed this trip, although again through the mountains, I had not realised just how mountainous this place was and my mind often flashed back to, I think, the early '70s when a plane full of UK tourists perished as their plane hit the mountain. I am reliably told by JR, that was when everyone flew to the north of the island. The airport we now use being a much more recent addition. He added that in winter it was often covered by snow, hard to comprehend in late October, when still in the 90s. The golf course is on a headland that simply appears to drop into the ocean making the drive down unbelievably spectacular.

Again we are met with an absolutely fantastic club-house and facilities. The course, whilst not a replica of Tecina, is very similar but flatter and I would suggest probably more difficult, with stunning vistas from virtually every vantage point. The back nine are, in my opinion, particularly enjoyable, especially thirteen through to sixteen, which are all right down near the coast-line. Greens were a touch slower and less undulating than Tecina but the course is again a must for any golfer visiting the island. It did provide an interesting development, which nearly caused abandonment of the whole competition. The tenth and twelfth tees are next to each other and the fairways run parallel down to the sea. The big arrow some 110

'Fore!' at Buena Vista.

The Sixth Tee at Amarillo.

yards below the tee which says ten, really gives you a clue which line to take. The last group out, the four leaders, inexplicably played down the twelfth, then realising their mistake, drove back and played the tenth, so in effect played twelve twice. The nineteenth was then in complete uproar as they should have been disqualified. However, as JR's youngest son, Jack, and JR's brother, Norman, were in the group, this was unlikely to happen. Anyway, for the rest of us, the opportunity for the rest of the week, and I have to say ever since, to tarnish the 'Vista Four' as cheats was too good to miss!

That night back into town, I do have to admit Playa has some quality restaurants because we ate unbelievably well. Be careful if you visit town to remember where you park. This night, young John, JR's eldest son, took us in but at the end of the night could not remember where he had parked the car and we had a three-hour wait until he spotted it long after everyone else had headed off home.

The final round was at the long-established course of Amarillo. This is one of the oldest courses in Tenerife, particularly popular with the English ex-pat community. Although on the coast as well, it did not have as many scenic holes

Sunset at Buena Vista.

Presentations, JR Classic.

as the other two earlier courses. In 2006, when we were there, it was like playing on a building site, as new houses and villas were being built along many fairways, which I have no doubt will sell in time for a fortune and eventually enhance the course.

The best hole was the short par three, sixth, at 120-yards carry over the ocean. Slasher was robbed of a hole-in-one here we were later told by observers. Kenny hit an eight iron beyond the flag and it rolled down the slope to the hole and appeared to us from the tee to be in, although the reaction of four or five walkers on the beach watching the golf clearly indicated it was not. When we arrived on the green, Kenny's ball was an inch from the hole, the pin however had not been placed in properly and apparently was leaning on the edge of the hole and had stopped Ken's ball from rolling into the cup. He tapped in for a birdie two, suitably pissed off and even more so when I rolled in a thirty-footer for the same score.

That night we went back into town and young John lost the car again. This time we were all sure where he parked it, but it was gone. It had been impounded by the police because he had parked it on the kerb. There then followed two days of mayhem trying to release the car which belonged to JR's neighbour who had lent it to him but was back in the UK. The Spanish authorities would not release it to anyone bar the registered owner, so this left us a car short and some, including Slasher, without their golf bags which had been in the boot.

My final round was at the Golf de Sur complex, three loops of nine on a course used in the past for a PGA event, the Tenerife Open, and famous for its bunkers with volcanic black sand in them. The course does have a championship feel about it. It was undeniably the most difficult of all the four courses I played. It has apparently remained the island's most popular and premier course and it's easy to see why. I birdied the seventh, fortified by two San Miguels offered over John's fence and despite the continual barracking as I stood over my fifteen footer.

Without doubt, Tenerife offers everything a group of lads could want from a golfing trip. The golf was good, if not exceptional. Sadly, these idyllic isles have developed the Costas' malady of slow play. I used to think it was because of the sun and heat, but it is not a problem in Florida. If visiting, I would recommend staying in a villa as opposed to a hotel, because food and entertainment are so readily available everywhere.

Do not just golf locally, but make an effort to get out to La Gomera and Buena Vista. It certainly enhances the whole Canary Islands experience.

4. England and Wales

The Belfry

The De Vere Belfry was a decent four-star venue for corporate events in the 1970s, with one good course, the Brabazon, and one average, the Derby. The resort was catapulted into mega status with a trio of Ryder Cups being held there in the 1980s, and again in 2002, with the popularity of the resort increasing in direct relationship to the increased recognition of the Ryder Cup as one of the premier sporting contests in the world. The development of a third course, the PGA National, and the basing of the PGA headquarters at the Belfry further enhanced its status in British golfing folklore.

In truth, whilst the golfing facilities have improved beyond all recognition, the hotel's facilities are still somewhat dated and it certainly needs some significant expenditure to bring it up to a standard more suitable for such a venue.

The hotel has adequate rooms/facilities but is not exceptional. The Bel-Air, a cheesy nightclub which attracts a rare cross-breed of Birmingham *haute couture* as well as the hotel residents, remains the main focal point of the evening entertainment for golfers. Two other bars and two fine restaurants together with a well-equipped spa and pool area complete the facilities and give adequate value for money in what is now an outdated establishment in need of refurbishment.

On one visit, I witnessed, as subsequently reported in the *News of the World*, a set-to between some stars of soapland and some locals. That day had featured a charity event on the Brabazon at which many of the stars of *Coronation Street, Eastenders* and *Emmerdale* had participated. That evening, one voluptuous, buxom local had asked 'Ashley Peacock' from Corrie for his autograph, but she wanted her bust signed. This he did, but her boyfriend went off on one. Ashley's brother (or bodyguard) was a boxer and defended him from a verbal assault which clearly was on the verge of becoming physical. He planted one on the boyfriend and it all went off. To say the following action was handbags at dawn would not be quite correct – there were one or two hefty blows being thrown about. However, watching as a bemused bystander, what was funny was how the characters reacted as one would expect from their TV persona. Les Battersby, aka Bruce Jones, just waded in, Curly Watts stood by simply avoiding the confrontation. It was hilarious. When I arrived home, I was greeted by the missus with said copy of the *News of the World* and asked for an explanation.

The Belfry clubhouse.

As a golfing venue, the develop-ment of the National means a visit to the Belfry can now feature two fine rounds, not just one, and a weekend is a much more enjoyable experience playing two entirely different types of course with differing challenges.

The Brabazon offers any golfer the opportunity to mimic the great Ryder performances and shots of the past. Particularly the short tenth and the opportunity to attempt to drive the green, and the eighteenth over water twice, where so many of the USA's great hopes ended in the drink.

I have to say that had the Ryder Cup not been played here, I think the course would not be as widely acknowledged as a must-play. In 200l, we played the week after the Ryder Cup should have taken place – it had been cancelled of course because of 9/11 – but the course was still set up for the event. Stands still in place, the rough had not been cut back and greens were extremely slick. I have played here four times but I would say that this time, was was the only memorable occasion, all because of the set-up, enjoyed out of a tragedy.

The start of the Brabazon is extremely staid for a supposedly great course. Two straight, basic par fours, bunkered fairways and green. Keep on the carpet, low iron in, good birdie opportunities. The course starts to liven up on the third, a fire par five, slight dog-leg left. This is a rare breed of par five which offers a great challenge to both pro and amateur. The drive has to hit the fairway and the pro would then would have a long carry over water to a narrow green bunkered front and back. Amateurs still have a third over this water with a lower iron, which has to be perfect to avoid sand. Any problem off the tee and a big number is a probability. Holes four to six are fine par fours. Like most of the holes on the course, all are difficult driving holes with approaches over water and all greens heavily protected with bunkers. The par three seventh is a spectacular looking hole over a large bowl of a bunker prior to the green. This has wrecked my card on more than one occasion. The eighth is similar to the other holes on the course. A recurring problem, I would suggest.

The ninth is tasty, with a wonderful approach to a water-protected hole. The drive again has to be very accurate to allow an attack at the pin. My mate, Ralph, in our 2004 visit hit, his drive ten yards into the little pool on the left of the tee, there merely as a visual enhancement to the course. Amazingly, at the next, the tenth, he then drove the green at over 300 yards. Such is the magnificence and uncertainty of golf. The magnificent driveable tenth urges one to take the challenge of driving the green.

Naturally, the tenth is the signature hole. You can either play as two irons or go for broke. We had always agreed to play a Mulligan here, have one go for the green, then inevitably play proper (i.e. safe). The eleventh is another Brabazon fine par four; the twelfth a long par three all over water, thirteenth another trademark par four; the fourteenth an average par three; the fifteenth is a fine par five; the

Par three, twelfth at the Belfry.

sixteenth another trademark four, before a great finish at seventeen and eighteen. The seventeenth is a great dog-leg par five. Reachable in two for the pros, three fine hits for us. The corner can be cut off but the risk-reward ratio is great. The final hole has of course been the star of many Ryder Cups. An extremely long par four, with a dog-leg left. The drive over water rewards the brave, taking the longer carry shortens the approach to an elongated three-tier rising green, again carrying water. Shortening the drive lengthens the approach, and brings into play fairway bunkers.

On the fairway of the eighteenth is a plinth celebrating C. O'Connor's cup-winning approach. Of course, you all have a go, generally ending up in water. The course has probably half a dozen quality holes: three, nine, ten, fifteen, seventeen and eighteen, the rest being much of a sameness, but the chance to replicate Ryder Cup heroes is one most golfers cherish.

I like the PGA National, because in my view, it is not as manufactured, holes are distinctly dissimilar and whilst of course, it does not have the history, I have always thought the course is possibly in better condition than its more famous cousin. There are again some exceptional holes. I like the par five second, as well as the fourth and fifth which offer brave rewards for water-risking drives. The finish from sixteen to eighteen is again a rare test.

To really get the benefit of the resort, it is essential to play both courses to enhance the experience. Also, give some consideration to extending the stay so as to sample some of the Midlands' excellent facilities. We have incorporated a stay at the Forest at Arden, in many ways superior to the Belfry. The course is used for the English Open and modern facilities to match at just one hour from the Belfry, make this a logical choice for an extended break.

I understand that the De Vere group are about to dispose of the Belfry and it is hoped the new owners invest in the infra-structure behind the golfing facilities and bring the whole resort up to a standard befitting its history and status.

Royal St David's & Nefyn

I had never played golf in Wales before I attended the Leasowe Golf Society Biennial Golf Trip to Harlech. This involved staying at the Harlech Castle Hotel, overlooking the Royal, for the weekend and playing at the Royal and the much-vaunted Nefyn just up the coast. The hotel is in a fine spot and the views, if the weather had been clear, would have been stunning. The hotel is basic and the town of Harlech much too quiet for a lads' trip. We had to travel out for any entertainment – mainly down the coast to Barmouth, which was a touch livelier. Despite the weather, the golf was nevertheless quite good.

The country's two leading championship courses are the celebrated Royal Porthcawl links, west of Cardiff, and Royal St David's, set in the shadow of the World Heritage-listed Harlech Castle. Whilst Porthcawl is an outstanding course, Royal St David's, which is surrounded by monstrous dunes but routed across much flatter ground, is fairly tame compared to the better links available elsewhere in Britain. It is not as good or as difficult as some of the lesser-known links courses such as Wallasey, West Lancs, etc. It can be described as a pleasant course which does not overtire as it is very flat. Like many links, its main defence is the wind.

Much more noteworthy is the remarkable Nefyn and District Golf Club which is set atop a high plateau that was sprayed with sand centuries ago and now features the crumpled fairways and humps and hollows of traditional beachside links. Nefyn is on a headland with the most stupendous views. When we played, the weather was horrendous. The first hole's drive had to be played at forty-five degrees to bring the ball back into the fairway. It was so bad that Slasher and Mike did not make it to the first tee. Russ and I completed ten, but the sight of our pals playing snooker in the club-house proved too much and we gave up. The last eight are on the peninsula and are the cream of the course, so I returned two days later in good weather to truly enjoy this wonderful place.

The following extract is taken from *Planet Golf* and truly does this wonderful course justice:

Nefyn – the headland.

The course is situated on the isolated Lleyn Peninsula and is reminiscent in scale and scenery of the Old Head of Kinsale. Nefyn & District is an unconventional golf club that was first founded as a village nine-holer in 1907. The course was then extended to eighteen in 1912, before J. H. Taylor and James Braid were asked to revise the layout in the 1930s and add an additional nine holes. Strangely, only 26 exist today: ten outward holes, apparently by Taylor & Braid, and two inward sets of eight.

With two distinct landforms, the early part of the Old Course is set along a vast coastal headland while its final holes occupy a tiny promontory that protrudes out from the peninsula and rises several hundred feet into the Irish Sea. The round begins with a downhill par four played toward the coast, which is followed by a four hole stretch that dramatically hug its cliffs. The most noteworthy of the holes along the headland is the almost world-class 2nd, which features a thrilling drive over the corner of the cliffs and a green perched high and close to its edge. With a more formidable greenside bunker and an angled green, this hole would be terrific and provide a real advantage for those driving nearer the sea. The solid 3rd, 4th and 5th holes also run alongside the ocean, but from the 6th the course turns away from the water and returns to the central clubhouse with the remainder of the front ten fairly pedestrian.

Nefyn – the view to the clubhouse.

Part of the original short course and located on their own spectacular spit of land, the final eight holes, by contrast, are far from mundane and feature a mix of mad and magnificent golf moments. The 11th, for instance, is a short par four where the only play is to hit a middle-iron into the base of a steep hill followed by a wedge up into a blind bowl. Even more unusual is the par five 12th, its blind drive seeming to plunge straight into the sea, the fairway beneath not apparent unless you walk down the hole the confirm its existence. A busy beach road and huge bottomless pit then lurk down the left side of a heavily left-sloping fairway, with smashing the ball up near the green in two about the only way to keep in play. More conventional is the brilliant clifftop 13th, which is played obliquely along a narrowing ridge, your drive needing to flirt with the ocean and a massive ravine in order to set up a decent shot into a small target squeezed into the Penisula's rocky tip. From here the course turns back for homewith the par five 17th, which overlooks the earlier headlands, the most memorable of the closing holes.

In many ways Nefyn is the archetypal Welsh golf course, a fun layout in a stunning location let down by some ordinary design. The golf does get breathtaking in places, but a number of potentially great holes are spoilt by rudimentary greens and bunkers, many being flat, uninteresting and offering straightforward recoveries.

Regardless of whether this general lack of polish, or the odd mediocre hole, affects your enjoyment of the round, the attractions of Nefyn are nevertheless apparent to all who play here.

I would advise any visitor to North Wales to try and play the Nefyn. Don't bother if the weather is too bad as there is simply no respite from it and it becomes far too difficult. Also ensure you play the inland eight on the peninsula and not the newer eight which, although pleasant, does not bear comparison to the eight out on the headland and, to be honest, is the main reason to play this course.

5. South Africa

In 2004, whilst on a business trip to South Africa, a work colleague not normally interested in our great game, advised me to visit Kimberley Golf Club, where he told me there was a museum dedicated to 'some kinsman of yours who could play a bit.'

Intrigued, I contacted the club and was informed that they did have a museum to celebrate the life of one Frederick Guthrie Tait. Now I was totally bamboozled but after visiting the club, I am able to tell you all about our Freddie and how it came to pass that a club based in the Diamond Centre of South Africa is now his spiritual home.

F. G. Tait was born in Edinburgh in 1870, the son of P. G. Tait, a distinguished professor at the city's university. Indeed, his Dad would be no stranger to historians of the game, for he is credited with the first-ever night round of golf, when he and several colleagues played with luminous balls around St Andrews, a round sadly terminated when one of his playing partner's gloves suddenly went up in flames. However I digress. Freddie became interested in golf at the age of five. His father and brother played golf regularly at St Andrews, and his brother, noticing the disappearance of his golf balls set a trap. The culprit was young Freddie, who had not taken the balls to play with, but had buried them. Apparently, he had watched the gardener planting potatoes and seen the resultant crop. He thought this was an appropriate way to increase his number of balls!

At seven, he played for the first time at the links, of which several years later, he would become the course record holder. Up to the age of twenty when he joined the army full-time, Freddie was a prodigious amateur and kept a meticulous record of all his rounds. Later, J. L. Low (whom Freddie beat in the last four of the British Amateur) would carefully document these in Freddie's biography. Tait is credited with introducing the game to the armed forces in 1890 and is generally accepted as being the finest-ever proponent of the game in the forces. Later that year, he broke the course record at St Andrews for the first time with a seventy-seven. In 1899, he broke it again, this time with a seventy. During this period, he also held the course records at Muirfield and Carnoustie amongst others.

Kimberley Golf Club.

At the peak of his prowess, he won many major amateur competitions – the Calcutta Cup, the St George's Cup (three times) and the Jubilee Vase. His major successes were at the British Amateur Champion-ships, which he won in 1896, when he crushed the then considered invincible H. Hilton by eight and seven in the final. He had already taken care of the famous John Ball in the quarters five and four. He won again in 1898, again taking care of Hilton and Low. In 1899, he played a memorable final against Ball, losing on the thirty-seventh, the first extra hole.

Kimberley Golf Club.

In the British Open, he finished third twice and was the leading amateur twice. By the turn of the century, he was probably playing his best golf. Low describes him as 'playing strokes outside the power of ordinary men' and 'as arguably the best putter of his generation.' Indeed, he once smashed a drive over 341 yards at the thirteenth at St Andrews with a carry of over 250 yards. This caused some consternation to his father, who had earlier that year stated in a scientific journal that it was impossible for any golf ball to carry more than 190 yards! His very last match at golf saw him beat Ball, winning one up.

So how come Freddie is now so revered in South Africa? Well in late 1899, Freddie and his unit, the famed Second Battalion, The Royal Highlanders (The Black Watch), arrived in Cape Town to 'sort out the Boers.' Sadly on 7 February 1900, Freddie died in battle at Koedoesburg Drift, five kilometres from Kimberley. In his will, he left his putter 'to the golf club closest to his place of death,' which by a geographical and historical quirk of fate, happened to be at Kimberley – a most worthy home of the putter and of the museum. Entering the club-house, you immediately see a poignant cross and reminder of Tait, together with a large boulder removed from the battlefield, next to what is described as a 'bluey'. In Kimberley and the surrounding district this is what a green was called up until 1960. The blue ground is diamondiferous pulsator gravel and was supplied by the famous De Beer Company which is based here. You are invited to try and putt on it and that was some experience in itself. Inside, there is a wondrous display of antique clubs and balls, trophies and pictures. Interestingly, I note that Tony Jacklin once held the course record here and in 1990 Ernie Els won his first pro-title here. The highlight is of course Freddie's putter.

Whilst in the club, I happened upon Mr Dave Wilson, curator, barman and general 'Mr Golf'. Amazingly, he simply took out the putter, marched me to the eighteenth and invited me to have a go. Bear in mind this putter is valued at over £50,000. Nervously I pushed the putt from about ten feet, slightly right. Nothing to do with the club, that's my normal problem! Dave then casually informed me that it was the Tait weekend and asked if I would like to play in the Stableford dedicated in Tait's name? So on Saturday I returned, playing off a ten handicap, I scored thirty-four points and was generally delighted. The course is not long, but tight, and in exquisite condition. At the end of the round suitably pleased, I retired to the nineteenth with my new friends. I am well-travelled but the nineteenth at Kimberley is simply without parallel for its warm welcome, super surroundings, great beer (essential) and fine food. Feeling a bit tipsy, (we were one of the early starters), I noticed a commotion on the eighteenth.

'Come on mate,' my new friends shout 'we are playing for the putter and diamond.' It transpires that at the close of the day, all contestants can enter the Tait Putting Competition, using Tait's actual putter. As can be seen from the following press release, history will forever show that I won the event and diamond!

Wigan Golfer Nets a Sparkler

Standish Court member, Ian Halliwell, became the first overseas winner of the Freddie Tait Putter at Kimberley Golf Club in South Africa last weekend. The Putting Competition is the highlight of the Tait Festival Weekend and the winner receives a De Beer diamond. Tait, a famous Scottish golfer of the 1890s was twice Amateur Champion and twice leading Amateur in the Open and was generally accepted to be the best putter of his generation. Tait died outside Kimberley in the Boer War and left his putter to the club. Valued at over £50,000, since 1936 it has been annually played for at the Tait Weekend.

Ian explains, at the end of the Final Stableford Competition, the Club Captain ceremonially brings out the putter. Every player has one putt with the Tait putter and the nearest to the Pin would win the Competition and the Diamond. When Ian played there had already been one hole in one and he made it two by curling the 30ft left to right putt, right into the centre. From over 200 puts, there were six successful putts resulting in a play off. Ian going second, putted dead length to six inches and none of the other participants came remotely close to taking the title of the Wiganer.

It was a remarkable feeling says Ian. To actually be on the Club Board which contains no lesser names than Tony Jacklin, who held the course record and Ernie Els who won his first professional title here is truly amazing. The Diamond literally was the icing on the cake.

Since then, I have become a Patron to the Museum donating artefacts from my travels that are pertinent to Freddie – pictures, postcards, tobacco cards, pottery as well as signed photos of modern golfers. I am proud of my association with this great club. Freddie is also permanently remembered each year at the South African Open where the leading amateur receives the Freddie Tait Medal.

If you are ever in this neck of the woods, make sure you sample the hospitality of this wonderful club. Soak in the history at the museum and enjoy a wonderful course. You will have done something the legendary Tait never had the opportunity to do, play a round in South Africa and you will remember it always.

FREDDIE TAIT PUTTING COMPETITION

THIS COMPETITION WILL TAKE PLACE ON THE
18TH GREEN AT THE CLOSE OF PLAY
'THE FLOATING TROPHY WILL BE UP FOR GRABS'
'THE WINNER WILL RECEIVE A DE BEERS CENTENARY *DIAMOND'*
[ONLY THE FAMOUS TAIT PUTTER MAY BE USED]

ENTRY FEE R5.00

Following on from my visit in March, I returned to Kimberley in October for the annual Barney Barnato, a week-long festival of golf, fun, ribaldry and revelry. This competition, named after one of the town's most famous sons from the Tait era is an eight-day tournament of separate individual daily Stablefords, culminating in an overall champion. We visited, and have done subsequently, on the last weekend. Each night, there is different cabaret and entertainment and players visit from all over Africa to take part in the fun. Being located next to Sun International's Flamingo Casino ensures that this is a memorable trip for the boys. In 2004, I was playing the best golf of my life, off eighteen. I was a bandito and quietly confident of scoring well. In the Thursday competition, I carded forty-two points and was confident of a place, but in the excitement Skitty and I had not signed the cards and were disqualified. I would have won a digital camera, DVD and video recorder, as well as the trophy – I was gutted! The next day I returned and produced quite simply the best round of my life, I holed everything, shot eighty and scored forty-four points. I had won the Friday Konica Sponsored Competition. Ensuring the cards was correctly signed, I later that evening collected my prizes – a generator and welding equipment. How I was supposed to get

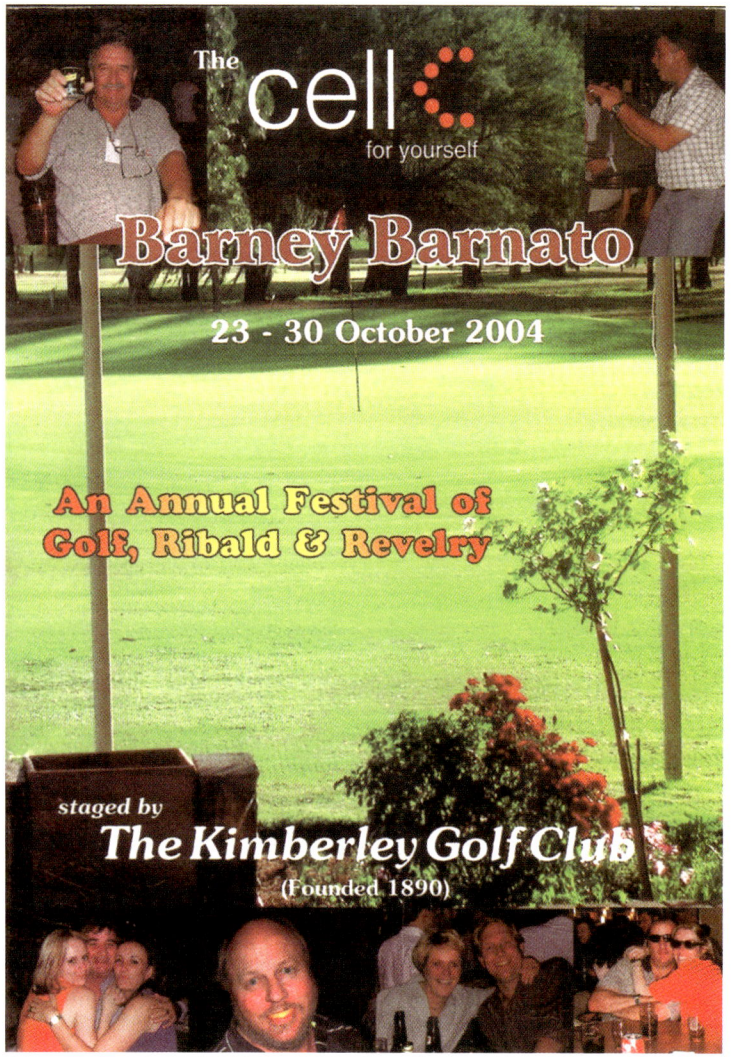

that through customs I did not know. I later gave them to a friend at whose ranch we were staying. I had the title, that's all that mattered though. My handicap was rightly slashed to eight for the Saturday competition, but I still shot seventy-nine and thirty-seven points for tenth place.

We all had a hole-in-one this week 'of sorts'. Kimberley is the home of the big hole, a gigantic crater created by the diamond mining industry, and the club cleverly arrange to take players out to hit a ball into the hole and accordingly issue a commemorative certificate. I got a hole-in-one in Kimberley. A really nice and inventive touch. John Chapman, however, got his by default – he missed a $1/4$ mile hole from only ninety yards, when his shot lipped out and stayed on the edge!

The next year, when we returned, Booty from Manchester, ensured the Friday Competition stayed in UK hands by winning with a forty-two point all. My defence of my title of my Barney handicap of eight was a brave one, I finished fourth with thirty-eight points. The Saturday of the competition, the last day, saw the weather take an awful turn. Thunder and lighting were everywhere, and I'm as apprehensive about this as is Lee Trevino.

In Africa, because the land is so flat, the skies light up very theatrically even if the bad weather is over sixty miles away. At the turn, whilst having our mid-round snack (in South Africa at every course we have played from Cape Town to Sun City, the players have to have a break – very civilised, two Castle beers and pie and chips, can't beat it!), the thunder seemed to our untrained ears to be getting closer. Speaking to Dave Wilson, the organiser, I asked whether we should go back out.

'Of course.' he said, 'there'll be a hooter if it's dangerous.' To which he added that the caddies, four young lads, will tell you before that, as they can sense it. Their ancestors have passed on that knowledge. It's self-preservation to them. Mike and Booty in the midst of two terrible rounds did not risk it; I went back out with Slasher Ken who was on course for a decent score. By the twelfth at the far end of the course, Slasher having hit a good drive asked for his six-iron, but got no reply. His caddy and mine were high tailing it back across the course like Ben Johnson and Linford Christie on heat! Taking heed of Dave's advice, we rapidly followed them, just reaching the club-house before a crack of lighting demolished a tree in the fairway to be followed by the hooter!

After the Barney, we headed back north to the customised resort of Sun City. This Vegas-style paradise is the home of the Nedved Million Dollar Challenge and was the perfect location to end our African adventure. When we arrived at the resort, we were directed to the awesome Palace Hotel, a stunning hotel which can only be described as magnificent. However, we were informed we were at one of the lesser hotels back down near the casino and entertainment complex. With more than a little disappointment, we reached the Cascade Hotel – an excellent base in its own right – but one which paled in significance when compared to the Palace. When we booked in, the receptionist took one look at four rough looking Englishmen, (we had been on the road for six hours after all) and announced there had been a cock-up with the booking. They had no twins left, just doubles. They proposed to let us have one night in the Palace and return back down the next day to the Cascades. We would all have taken that except Booty, who went off on one.

Teeing off over the crocs.

'If you think I am traipsing back here with my case tomorrow, you are very much mistaken. Where we go, we stay. Got that!' he stated very angrily.

He stands behind us, well over six-feet six-inches tall, and must have created quite an intimidating image. The outcome was, after more ranting and raving, we went back to the Palace where we stayed at no extra cost for the full four days. In all truth, this outstanding hotel was wasted on four lads, but we all returned next year with our spouses, when we realised that there was a water park, nature reserve, elephant sanctuary and several restaurants we had not noticed on the first visit. The place is quite simply awesome and so cheap with the exchange of the rand to the pound. Beer was less than £1 a pint, three-course meals and accompaniments were less than a tenner. Golf at two championship courses for less than £30 for the round, buggy, spotter/caddy, mid-round buffet.

We first played the Lost City Course, which I think this is a more spectacular course than the Gary Player, if not as difficult as its sister course which annually hosts the $1,000,000 Challenge and has recently hosted the last two Women's World Cups. The Lost City includes the fabled crocodile-pit hole, which now has four of my Titleists – but I have got my own back each time by having their cousin for tea that same evening. The first hole saw our spotter's head about 300 yards down the fairway, only to all have to march back after all four tee shots entered the bush at about 180 yards. These guys earned their money and were

of great help on the greens in particular. Slasher, Booty and I visited the sixth twice one day. We went for a balloon ride and the wind got up, forcing us off line and we crash-landed on the sixth fairway (not half tearing it up as we slid along!). Later on, as Slasher's superbly hit ball ended up in one of the basket marks, he claimed ground under repair. Not sure if he was right but we let him have it. This course has an awesome club-house, voted the best in South Africa, with stunning views back up the ninth and eighteenth fairways. It is always a place to see one or two stars; we have seen footballers Bruce Grobbelaar and Harry Kewell, and

Entrance to the Palace Hotel.

cricketers Lance Klusener and Sir Ian Botham – and they have met me! It is a great place to play and socialise.

The Country Club is certainly more of a challenge from a golfing perspective. From the pyramid-shaped hotel that dominates the skyline (The Cascades) to the lush opulent greens, it is plain to see the course is not just drenched in sun, but also in money. The course does house some impressive holes. The best is probably the ninth, a par five at 545 yards. The drive must be straight to avoid the trees on the left and large bunker on the right. The big hitters can reach the green in two but staying there is a different matter. The hole is a raised island and lies on the upper level of a split-level lake. Even for those laying up it is a difficult short iron approach. A par here is some accomplishment. The seventeenth and eighteenth with water on the drives and approach are a tremendous finish. You can get your picture taken with the Nedved Cup and examine the cards of all the winners over the year. The Yardage Books at both courses are worth buying as they include a preview of that year's challenge and the competitors.

With a casino and top class shows, the resort offers a 24-hours-a-day option for food, drink and entertainment. Considering the opulence of the resort, any UK visitor will find it unbelievably cheap to spend a week here, providing you don't blow it in the gaming halls.

If you are travelling to Sun City, it is about two hours from Johannesburg and the drive is not straightforward and unless you are used to South Africa can be quite intimidating in places. The resort does have buses available from the airport, so arrange these, or hire a limo, and start the holiday in style as we did with the ladies on our next visit.

With a caddy at Sun City.

With Mike and the Nedved Trophy.

Golf and My Stroke

Baseball, football, riding, polo, even lawn tennis abandon us or we abandon them as our wind gets shorter and our bones more brittle. But once a golfer, you are wedded to the game for life.
H. J. Whigham, *The American Golfer*

Golf is essentially one of those pursuits in which it is a hundred times better to have loved and lost than never to have loved at all.
Bernard Darwin, *Golf*

Once bitten, it is akin to having your neck punctured in Transylvania – there is no known antidote.
Martin Johnson

When you fall in love with golf, you seldom fall easy: It's obsession at first sight.
Thomas Boswell (1797–1858)

I love this game to death. It's like a drug I have to have.
Tiger Woods

Golf is not relaxation, golf is everything, golf is a philosophy, it's a religion absolutely.
Sir Bob Reid

When I look on my life and try to decide out what I have got most actual pleasure, I have no doubt at all in saying that I have got more out of golf than anything else.
Lord Brabazon

My worst day on the golf course still beats my best day in the office.
John Hallisey

It is a test of temper, a trial of honour, a revealer of characteristic.
David Robertson Forgan

… but I challenge anyone to dispute the fact that every good golfer will be at heart a good person.
Arnold Haultain

I've found that to be truly successful in the world of golf one must first come to accept oneself as a human being who has the inner capabilities to improve and become a better person.
Gary Player

6. A Bad Stroke

Monday, 18 December 2006, a week before Christmas, just any normal day, except it was the day that changed and redefined my life forever. We had returned from Florida one week earlier and that evening were scheduled to visit my favourite Indian restaurant, the Raj, to celebrate Chris, my daughter's boyfriend's twenty-first birthday. A year, which had included trips to South Africa, Tenerife, Gibraltar, Madeira and Florida, was about to end well. I felt indestructible and indispensible. At the end of the day, I would be neither again.

I drove to Chester completely unaware of the *maelstrom* about to explode and here, thank the Lord, I had my first bit of fortune of the day. If my stroke had happened just one hour earlier, it beggars belief to consider the carnage I could have caused on either the M6 or M56 on my journey in. I arrived at Chester, ordered a sausage sandwich and a coffee and was tucking in when I began to notice a problem with my left arm and hand. I could not pick up my phone or my papers, I went to the toilet and was unable to unzip my flies or straighten my tie. Slowly, it seemed as if my whole left side was being unzipped from me. I had in the previous months made every office appoint a first-aider and this proved to be money well spent at Chester. Office Manager, Lisa Burke, took one look at me and phoned the hospital and ordered an ambulance. Her quick thinking was to prove pivotal to my longer-term recovery. Then the left-hand side gave way completely; I could not stand or move my arm, my speech was slurred. I was not in any pain at all, but I was fully aware of my predicament. My father had died of a stroke in 2000 and I was sure I was having one myself. I was not at this stage afraid, that would come later. Having had a brain tumour and catching meningitis subsequent to its removal, I knew what pain was and I certainly was not in it.

The ambulance came and took me to the Countess of Chester Hospital. I am told I was still eating my sandwich during this trip. I do not recollect a great deal of the next fortnight. I remember Karen in tears at my bedside and me promising to be home for Christmas, at the same time she had been told by the consultant that the next few days were critical. She was told to keep her phone with her at all times. My stroke had been caused by high blood pressure of 200 over 140 when I was first tested. The problem was that the bleeding did not stop for several days. This apparently would inevitably lead to further damage and the main concern was my heart. I was monitored continually during these first few days. Christmas came and went, New Year too. A pretty miserable time for Karen, the kids and the family, but New Year was to bring more optimism. Having obviously got over the worst, it appeared my life was no longer in imminent danger, but for every cloud there were not many silver linings. For even with the bleed apparently now under control and my blood pressure falling, there had been significant damage and the family had to now give some consideration to the fact that I may be permanently disabled. Of course I heard the whispers and tried to remain confident. The hospital staff were all imperious, ever-cajoling, encouraging, helpful and confident, in particular that I would play golf again.

I only needed to look around the ward to see that I had again been very fortunate. Compared with most others on the ward, I was in the best shape. I could speak, see and my memory and faculties had not been damaged. The arm and leg were not functioning, but all told me that this could be worked on.

The hospital was capable of giving highly humorous moments that were priceless. An older gentleman in the next bed had had a small stroke which clearly affected his memory. The occupational therapists always test new patients with a brief who is this with a variety of photos. On showing him some, he clearly did not have a clue who Tony Blair was, The young nurse told him it was the Prime Minister at which he pointed at Margaret Thatcher and exclaimed, 'there's the bitch and I didn't vote for her.' He was then asked what month and year it was. 'August 1979,' he replied 'and it's been a shit one so far.'

You shouldn't laugh but I was in stitches. He was also a diabetic but had five sugars in his tea and on everything. I pointed this out to his wife who advised me that he had only been diagnosed in 2004. He also had a hearing aid and he believed that the hospital had stolen his battery. One day he leant over to me, 'Bloomin' National Health, cannot trust it under the Tories. They're that short of money they've pinched my battery and won't replace it. And guess what, I've bloody caught diabetes apparently while I have been here.'

I had started physiotherapy on a daily basis. It was the highlight of my day, and was the only time I could do something to help myself. Visiting remained pivotal to my recovery and, despite the long journey from Wigan to Chester, Karen was a constant source of strength to me. I was never short of company as friends and family rallied around and I will be forever in their debt. Karen started massaging my bad leg and slowly there were signs of movement buoyed by the exceptional work by the physios.

I still had doubts whether I would walk again and occasionally bouts of depression would kick in. A big turning point for me came in early January whilst at a particularly low ebb. I believed that in my sleep I was visited by my dad. Now of course, you may not believe this is possible. Yes, it could have been me contriving a dream to suit my purpose. Whatever, I felt my dad tap my shoulder and look down at me and comment, 'come on son, we're not ready for you yet, there's lots of unfinished business for you here.' With that, he lightly kissed my head and walked away, giving me that look he had always mastered, a scolding glance that showed affection but chastised at the same time. I have always mastered the latter if not the former with my kids. Waking up, I felt re-envigorated. I assumed that he was on about looking after the kids, being a granddad myself one day, but over the next six months, two events gave greater significance to his comments. In spring, my wife, having had problems for several years which had been diagnosed as shingles to Carpel Tunnel Syndrome, was told she had apparently been suffering from MS for years. The same week, my mother at seventy-three years of age was diagnosed with breast cancer. She had undergone a mastectomy in 1990 and was to have another immediately. These are the two events I believe my father was now referring to and that no matter what my problems were, I needed to offer what support I could to my loved ones in his absence.

Whilst at Chester, I do believe I became a humbler, nicer person. I was not used to having to rely on anyone and now I needed help in eating and even going to the toilet. I had also had to hand over my business empire to my colleagues and quite clearly, I was not indispensible – life was going on as before in the real world outside my ward. There is something pretty humbling when a young girl, young enough to be my daughter, is wiping my arse for me.

Time dragged. January seemed an eternity, I had started to get some movement back into my legs; I could now access a wheelchair and stand up. Heather and the Pain Squad (the Physios) were quite confident I would now walk again, but there had still been no movement in my arm. I suspected they thought I had lost use of this forever, but fortune was to favour me again.

My main concern during this period was the constant smell of urine I seemed to have, that type of old man's smell caused by dribbling into the container and over my pyjamas. It's hard to control the flow and hold the container with just one hand. The nurses developed a type of catheter, a Durex type condom covered the penis and was connected by a tube to a bag to which I could freely urinate without a single drop escaping. This contraption was the reason I can now move my left arm and hand. One night whilst lying in bed asleep, I awoke with a start. I was licking my lips and someone was spraying water at me.

Opening my eyes I looked down and saw a fountain of urine spraying over me as the cover had slipped off. Without thinking, my left hand shot out and re-covered myself with the balloon. Amazingly, and in one second, my left arm and hand had reconnected themselves to my brain. Rapidly I got relative full movement back.

I had, despite receiving outstanding care at the unit in Chester, got a burning desire to move closer to home to Leigh Infirmary. Over the next two to three weeks, encouraged by the Pain Squad who had appointed themselves my escape committee, I had seen considerable advances in my strength and movement. Karen continued to give her overwhelming support and was continually contacting all the right people to facilitate the move back home.

There are too many people to thank, but they know who they are. I am eternally grateful. The hospital had one last trick to play on me. The ward sister came in one day and said, 'We need your bed so we are moving you closer to Wigan.' They did, from Ward 51 to 53, about twenty yards closer, but this was to be my last week in Chester and after eight weeks in the Countess of Chester, I was transferred to the Rehab Bridgewater Ward at Leigh Infirmary. Whilst delighted to be back in Wigan, where the pressure on the

family travelling would not be as great, I was sad to leave the staff at Chester who had become close friends, confidantes, and I hope will remain so for years to come. I was elated in September to be able to invite a number of the staff to a cocktail evening at the Golf Day I organised for the Stroke Association. In truth, it was only a small gesture of thanks to those who had helped my recovery in my darkest hours, but I hope this becomes a regular date. I am delighted to say I have also accepted the position of Chairman for the hospital's Fundraising Committee which will allow me to keep in touch with these exceptional professionals. At Bridgewater, my recovery continued and within two weeks I was walking unattended and looking forward to coming home.

I was faced now with other problems. Having recovered somewhat physically I needed counselling to prepare me for the residual damage I would inevitably carry forward to future years. I also needed to ensure I took whatever means and support was available to reduce the likelihood of further illness. Here I received considerable help from the Wigan Stroke Association and in particular, Jim Brown, who spent many hours discussing with me how my life could move on. I initially had to try and accept what had caused my stroke to happen. Everyone seemed to believe

Ian back golfing at Standish.

my hectic lifestyle, 100 hour weeks, running half a dozen businesses were not conducive to a long life. I had been overweight, but the time in hospital had alleviated that, I had dropped from eighteen stone to fifteen stone in three months. I had never smoked, so providing I took my medication, and was tested regularly, there was no reason why my blood pressure should not remain under complete control. My business interests had coped in my absence so I could now spend less time at work. Jim convinced me that actually by surviving the stroke I had now a much longer life expectancy. I think there's little doubt that I was a ticking time bomb and that at a different time and place I may not have survived. 2007 was to have been a year with many special occasions. In April, my nephew was to marry in Paris; in May, Karen would turn fifty; in June, Emma would be twenty-one and would graduate later that year. I quickly realised that focusing individually on these events would give my life renewed vigour and purpose. I am delighted to say I was able to attend and enjoy all these family highlights. There had to be changes and we had to do things differently. Rather than flying to Paris, we went on Eurostar and it showed me the considerable difficulties disabled people have in travelling. I was still weak at this stage, although fully mobile. Lifting cases was a problem. Trying to get from Euston to Waterloo was a nightmare for Karen who was doing her best to look after me. By comparison, the trip in France was a doddle. I think it's a culture thing, but the word for a stroke in French is *l'attack*. This conveys much more seriousness and *'J'ai l'Attack avec hyper tension,'* always got a prompt response from every Parisian we encountered as opposed to 'my husband's had a stroke' here in the UK, which simply achieved looks of indifference. What I quickly learned was that if you don't look ill in this country, there is little help offered. At Eurostar for example, when the case was going through the check, the attendant said he could not touch my case and I had to lift it myself. This was an impossibility, and he watched without lifting a finger whilst Karen did it for me. Karen wanted to visit Cornwall for her fiftieth. Now, in the past I would simply have driven, but not now. She had to share the responsibility, not easy for someone who had never driven on a motorway before. Later on in the year, in Florida, she had to drive abroad for the first time, a further example of how an illness affects your partners as well as yourself.

Slowly my strength was returning. I still had bad days, I would tire easily but reorganising my work life and schedule (travelling to work by train instead of car) certainly aided my recovery. I cannot take my drink, the tablets clearly kick in and any meaningful night out has to be followed by a day in bed recovering. I also got back on the golf course and decided to use this interest in facilitating a stroke awareness campaign and allowing fundraising activities for the Stroke Association. This would now become a key focus to enable my life to move forward. Later that year, I would participate in the National Par Three Championships, organise my own Celebrity Golf Classic and in the process, raise more than £12,000 to date. In 2008, I would complete my aim to play on every continent and further raise the Stroke Association's profile, continue to raise funds and also become involved more in Chester Hospital's Relative Comfort Campaign.

The stroke has given me an opportunity to make something more of my life. I am no longer frightened of future strokes. When I first left hospital, every ache and pain brought worries about further illness. I was always aware that there is a likelihood of future strokes, but I will do what I can to minimise the threat and in the meanwhile, try to enjoy a rare quality of life with my wonderful wife to whom I owe so much, and at the same time continue to offer support and comfort as appropriate to my family and friends. To continue, my stroke awareness golf campaign gives me a will and reason to live. Before I was very money- and asset-conscious, now I truly appreciate all I have and what it would mean to lose it. Life is very precious and precarious.

I still have aches and pains. My left side is still slow in relation to the rest of my body. My leg causes grief periodically. I read books and stupidly identify my condition with those that have been written about, (currently I think I have Dropped Foot Syndrome). When asked by the doctor how I feel, I usually reply, 'Uncomfortable not ill,' to which he often replies,

'We cannot do anything about discomfort, it comes with the territory.'

When you have an illness – and I have now had two major scares, (having a brain tumour at thirty-eight and a stroke at forty-eight – my aim is to be fifty-eight and as healthy as I am now. Nothing else really matters. Without good health, you are nothing. If along with this you have love and a great family life, want fiscally for nothing, then, despite all my problems, I will feel truly lucky and blessed.

There are always opportunities in life and I love waking up every morning. I have survived another day, what can I now do to make this day special. Survive it again. That's not negative, but a realistic approach to life – by surviving I hope I will be able to enhance the lives of those around me, develop myself as a person and become a better golfer.

You do need luck to recover. My stroke could have been far worse. My wife in particular, but all the family, put considerable effort into keeping my attitude right to my misfortune. Her love was the fuel to my recovery. Then there are the professionals in the Health Service of whom I stand in awe at their abilities, compassion and dedication. I simply acted with primeval instincts to survive and make a better future for myself, but without the above help I would have failed.

7. Nailcote Hall:
Home of the British Par Three Championship

Whilst in hospital, I had been given that greatest of modern golf monthlies *Punk Golf* to read. In it was advertised an event they were sponsoring, the British Par Three Championship, to be played at a gem of a small course at Nailcote Hall near Coventry. After I had proved to myself I could play again, I decided to apply to play in this tournament and started to research its history and find out a bit more about the event and course.

The course and event were the brainchild of local entrepreneur, businessman and hotelier, Mr Rik Cressman who took an old historic event – it had been first played for in 1933 – and in a short span, established it as a premier event on the circuit. By mixing the professional competition with a pro-am and celebrity-amateur competition, he attracted headline sponsorship including Sky Sports TV coverage. Without doubt, his finest achievement was the course itself which has become such a challenge even to the pros, but for the amateurs, it is certainly as good a test as one could face and in my opinion embodies all I want in a golf challenge. It truly is the ultimate test of a short game prowess.

The British Professional Short Course Championship has been steeped in the history of the game since it was first hosted at Torquay's Palace Hotel in 1933. The inaugural championship was graced by some of the all-time great players, including many past Open champions: Alex Herd, Alf Padgham, Ted Ray, J. H. Taylor and Harry Vardon. Peter Alliss' father, Percy, played in the event, as did Henry Cotton in later years and many other Ryder Cup players including Abe Mitchell (the personal tutor of Samuel Ryder) who is figured on top of the Ryder Cup Trophy.

The Modern Era from 1998

It is fitting that a past Ryder Cup star, Peter Baker, should be the first winner in the new era. For those who delight in the finesse and art of shot-making in golf, rather than the power driving of the modern age, the British Professional Short Course Championship is a welcome challenge of golfing skill.

In 1999, the championship was honoured by 1951 Open Champion, Max Faulkner, and twice Ryder Cup captain, Bernard Hunt. A thrilling competition was ultimately won by European Tour star, Carl Mason, thanks in no small measure to a stunning course record of a six under par twenty-one in the third round.

The 2000 event produced the first play-off when Jeremy Robinson, from the European Tour, defeated Brian Rimmer on the first extra hole after they had tied with a score of four under par.

2001 was a very special year celebrating the late Max Faulkner's fiftieth anniversary of winning the Open Championship and the Championship lived up to the special occasion in every way. Ultimately the title went to Midlands' star, Robert Rock, who won with a four under par score of 104, but only after a really exciting three-man play off.

The 2006 Championship celebrated the sixtieth anniversary in professional golf of two times Ryder

Cup captain, Bernard Hunt, and the competition that followed was special indeed. With the strongest field ever, including eighteen European Tour professionals such as Jarrod Moseley from Australia and Steve Scahill from New Zealand, the competition was fierce. After thirty-six holes, rising European Tour stars, Tom Whitehouse and Shaun Webster, tied at seven under par and after a birdie two on the seventh hole, Shaun Webster was crowned Champion.

The 2007 event broke new boundaries in terms of being the most high-profile tournament to date. Television and media exposure reached new heights including coverage on Sky Sports and there was the highest turn-out in relation to spectator numbers, celebrity numbers and participation by European Tour professionals. However, it was down to Steve Cowle to take the coveted title of 2007 Numark British Par Three Champion, finishing six under par, four shots ahead of second-placed Sam Walker. In doing so, he became the first non-European Tour professional to win the title. Steve wasn't finished there though, because he also won the Pro-Am team competition with his partner and former England Rugby Union International, Tim Stimpson.

In this year, I had the honour of playing with the legend and gentleman, Bernard Hunt. This was a dubious distinction, whilst the honour of playing with the most decorated player present was a significant coup for me and our Stroke Awareness campaign, I knew our chances of success were minimal in view of Bernard's age when compared with modern day pros such as Graham Storm, David Lynn, Philip Archer and numerous others straight from the European Tour (such was the significance of the event). Bernard had after all been winning tournaments before I was born – I subsequently found out he won the Egyptian Open in 1956 for example. However, the plus was the gallery that followed him around, and we were probably the most watched pairing, so I had a measure of his

Ian with golfing legend Bernard Hunt, MBE.

popularity and the respect which he was shown. If I was now unlikely to ever achieve my goal of playing on the circuit, then this was certainly no poor man's substitute. On arrival, I was given a player's badge, name on the leaderboard – yes that's my name on a PGA Board! I could not believe it.

'On the first tee, Ian Halliwell,' the announcer booms, you simply can't put a price on how magical it felt. From death's door to a *bona fide* PGA event, life cannot get any better. Of course you can put a cost on it, about the same as a week in the Algarve or Costas. No comparison, this wins every day. As I later wrote in *Punk Golf*, to participate in the event was a pleasure; to play with Bernard an honour, and even with all my other travels and successes in Africa, Florida and Australia, this was 'The One', the experience of a lifetime. Since then, I have had the opportunity to return many times as part of my preparation for the 2008 event. I know the course inside out, have managed to break thirty, but I am fully aware the greens in August will offer another considerable test. That a course of nine par three holes, total length 1,031 yards, can bring so many quality players to their knees is however the main strength of the event. Rik and his staff have created a small course of major golf standard. To hit the greens is not sufficient, to hit them in the right place and stop on is some achievement.

Hole 1: *The Warren, 116 yards*

The first hole is a tougher introduction to the Cromwell course than it first appears. The green is long and narrow with run-offs to the bunkers which protect it on both sides and the back of the green. A really accurate shot to the heart of the green is essential to achieve a good result. I think you must hit the front of the green, anything past or left or right and par is nigh impossible.

Hole 2: *Rhodies Bank, 114 yards*

This hole is usually the easiest hole on the course, but anything short brings the meandering ditch and two bunkers at the front of the green into play. Quite a few places where a chip from off the green doesn't present too many difficulties if you need to get out of trouble. Being raised, this green offers best chances of staying on. Good birdie opportunity. In 2007 gave up two holes-in-one, the only ones in the event.

Hole 3: *Baswich Brook, 124 yards*

An elevated tee presents a lovely view of this hole with the brook blended into the landscape and protecting the green on the left, so any shot pulled a bit can be in trouble. Bunkers at the front and back surround a sloping green with some tricky contours. Again, the ideal shot must be front edge to hold on the green.

Hole 4: *Emerald Isle, 87 yards*

Aptly named, the fourth is a tiny green shaped like an upturned saucer and demands a really precise tee shot or else! Out of bounds at the back is a big penalty for a slightly over-hit shot. It's a hole of

Hole four.

extremities, lots of birdies but also lots of bogeys and double bogeys. Everyone thinks it should be easy as the shortest hole, but it has a lethal reputation. I hit the green on all four occasions but never held it. Into the farmer's field twice.

The ninth – the significant hole.

Hole 5: Needle's Eye, 95 yards

The second shortest hole is a beautiful hole where players need to be really accurate to avoid the two huge oak trees which are only ten yards apart in front of the green. Touch them at your peril and the ball could be in the deep bunker at the front. More bunkers surround the green at the back so a long shot can run into trouble too. Beautiful hole but the bunker at the back seems to attract my ball like a magnet. When I played with Karen here, she got a par, her first ever. After hitting her approach just short, her chip hit the flag and she rollocked me for not taking it out. She then holed a fifteen-footer and her cheer could be heard back in Wigan.

Hole 6: Carp's Catch, 110 yards

Possibly the most attractive hole on the course with the elevated tee set under the trees with a fabulous view of the lake which threatens on the right for any sliced attempt. The green is a dish and the pin position can change the complexion and difficulty of the tee shot dramatically. A back pin adds the risk of out-of-bounds just a few yards away. They are putting a waterfall in, which will enhance the hole further. Aim left with a fade over the front bunker for a decent birdie opportunity. After her par, Karen lost three brand-new Callaways here, refusing to play with poor balls now after having a par.

Hole 7: Moulie's Bridge, 146 yards

Stroke index one and always used for hole-in-one car challenges, with good reason! The longest hole on the course is slightly uphill with an elevated green protected by a huge St Andrews-style bunker at the front. Get in it and the penalty can be easily more than one shot. The prevailing wind can add one or two clubs to what you think is needed to reach the green. If you land the green, the walk over Moulies bridge is very satisfying. Front bunker offers an impossible shot.

Hole 8: Twin Oaks, 106 yards

The last three holes are always testing and the eighth is always capable of wrecking a good scorecard. The green is a highly elevated small and relatively flat target, but any over-hit shot runs the risk of water at the back or another deep bunker like the seventh. The two oak trees near to the green add to a dramatic hole. I believe this is the hardest hole, and again I have never kept a ball on the green.

Hole 9: Nailcote Falls, 133 yards

The newly developed ninth hole has replaced a bunker at the front of the green with twenty-five

Hole Five.

yards of water, so with the pond at the back as well, it is nearly an island green like 'Sawgrass'. The oak tree on the right alongside the green means a lay up is not necessarily a safe or easy option, and there's sure to be some hearts broken whenever this hole is played. In 2007, one unlucky pro ran up thirteen here! I got a birdie here and at our works do, Dave Simister, got a hole-in-one to win our Christmas Trophy.

The course in late summer for the competition is set up by the greenkeepers as appropriate for such a major event. The course flora and fauna are in full bloom making the course a kaleidoscope of colour. The greens are as slick and in as good a condition as you could wish to find anywhere. Playing in the event, as I later wrote in *Punk Golf*, was the experience of a lifetime, but as I have revisited the course over winter as part of my build-up for next year, the whole Nailcote experience is also worthy of note. A fine hotel with excellent facilities and staff, enhance the golf experience.

As I am no longer, nor it has to be admitted ever was, the biggest hitter in the world, standing on a tee knowing I can reach the green always gets me going; that's why I love par threes and here at Nailcote are some of the best.

8. Carden Park: the MRC Golf Classic

I have, over the years, played in many celebrity amateur competitions and my office wall is covered with photos of these occasions. I have played with international footballers such as Ian Rush, Phil Neal and Trevor Cherry, snooker stars such as Dennis Taylor and Rex Williams, rugby stars like Andy Farrell and Dennis Betts. It seemed logical, therefore, to organise our own competition in order to raise awareness of stroke-related problems and raise funds for the Stroke Association. Utilising the offices of Allan Clark and the Celeb Golf Tour, we held ours in September 2007 at the prestigious Carden Park venue in Chester. Carden Park is a De Vere facility, but whilst its courses may not have the international recognition of the Belfry, the rest of the hotel and facilities far outstrip its Birmingham rival. There are two courses at Carden: the Nicklaus (not unsurprisingly designed by Jack) and the Cheshire. The Nicklaus is the longer and tougher of the two courses and has been used on many occasions to host PGA Events, most recently the English Seniors Open. We however chose the Cheshire, principally because the eighteenth green is majestically placed directly under the club-house veranda and guests could watch the action. We could also video everyone driving off the tenth and putting on the eighteenth as it was a shotgun start.

The Cheshire is one of those unique courses which begins with a par three. I had donated a prize of two weeks in Florida to the nearest to the pin. Ironically it was won with the first shot of the day by my team member, scratch golfer Phil Abbot. The course was as usual in supreme condition. Not one of the 120 golfers had anything but nice comments to make about the condition of the Cheshire. The back nine are particularly impressive, the eighteenth as a closing hole is gorgeous. Teeing off high up on a hill, you can see all down to the green in front of the club-house. At just over 300 yards, it invites you to have a go for it, but a pond just short can wreck the card unless you get the drive away 100%. All, I hope, had a fabulous day. The celebs as usual made themselves readily available to all the participants and I am always amazed at how much cheer these guys bring to a round of golf yet can remain so intensely competitive.

We had a couple of fun competitions on the day which raised funds and went down

Ian greets staff from Chester Hospital at Carden Park.

very well. I had a couple of wooden antique clubs from my Sports Bar days, a driver and a putter, both dated early twentieth century. Prior to the event, we had a putting competition where you had to use the old putter. I also went up to the eighteenth tee to hit a drive off, amazingly it went about 180 yards. All competitors were given a go with the wood and the nearest to me won the Chairman's Drive In. Unbelievably, two or three players actually still drove the green. One player drove the green with the antique to about ten feet, then with his £500 Taylor-made drove straight into the water. Sadly, he could not play his first.

The evening, as usual in these comps, was completed with a gala meal where the showbiz celebs royally entertained us. A marvellous day climaxed with us achieving our goal of raising £10,000. I was made up! The day before I had held a Pimms reception for the staff at Chester and this completed a worthy and marvellous two days. My team, with Willie Thorne starring, finished a creditable third, beaten (as was admitted in their winning speech) by dodgy handicapping. Former Sunderland footballer and Cup Winner, Micky Horswill, won the Celeb competition.

The success of the day has ensured we will return next year, and hopefully annually, with a bigger and better event featuring a Pro Event for the Halliwell Stroke Awareness Cup and a Pro-Am, followed the next day by the Celeb Team Competition. To all who supported my charity I am heavily indebted.

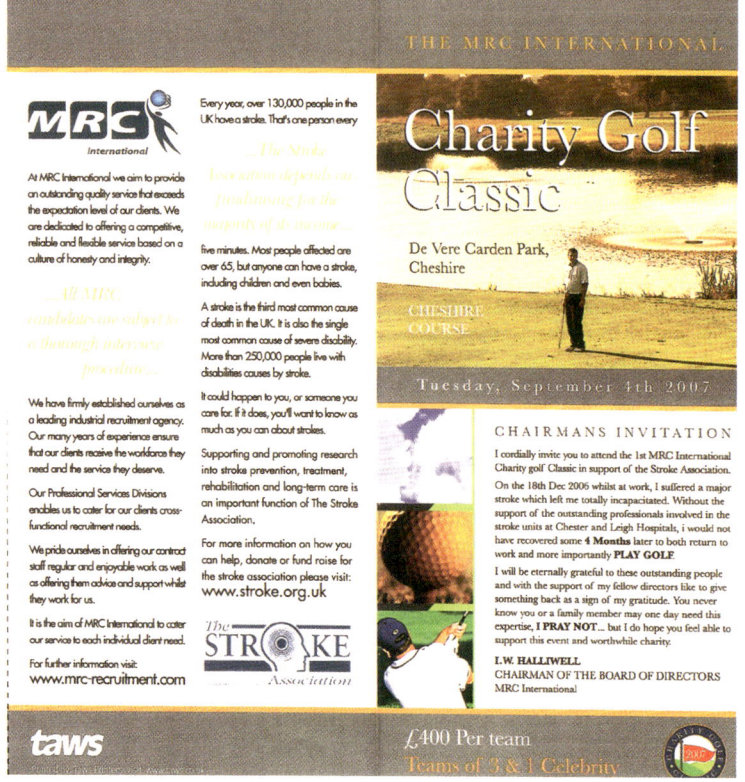

Golf with the wife and friends (post-stroke)

Being able to play in a beautiful setting is part of the essence of golf.
Arnold Palmer

It means … getting close to nature, fresh air, and exercise, a sweeping of mental cobwebs and a genuine relaxation of tired tissues.
David Robertson Forgan

Indeed the highest pleasure of golf may be that on the fairways and far from all the pressures of commerce and rationality, we can feel immortal for a few hours.
Colman McCarthy

Golf is like yoga for me, it has had wonderful, sedative, remedial qualities for my day to day life.
Ronnie Corbett

I consider it my particularly good fortune to be a part of a game that allows man or woman, teenager or octogenarian, to express their love for life in an arena bequeathed by nature.
Nick Faldo

Golfers belong to an exclusive universal club … their connection is not bound by time or geography. It is in the spirit and joy of the game.
J. P. Resnick

Winning has always meant much to me, but winning friends has meant the most.
Babe Didrikson Zaharias (1914–56)

The friends you make on the golf course are the friends you make for life.
Jessica Anderson Valentine

Golf may be, and is, used by people of every colour, race, creed and temperament, in every climate and all year round … thus has our happy game of golf wound a bright cordon round the world, and so does play her part in the great evolution of general contentment.
Henry Leach

Around the first old comrades are assembling … memories, like a scarlet thread running the frosted winter months, bind old rivalries to new challenges … your blood awakens as your hand grips the club, and once more you are alive and in love with life in the open.
Charles W. Moore

A leisurely round [of golf] with a close friend on a summer's evening comes close to the best of all human experiences.
W. F. Deed, *Weekend Telegraph*, 21 March 1998

9. Florida

Why would anyone not choose Florida as the ideal golfing destination? With the glorious weather, the quality and price of the golf courses available, and the location to keep all the family happy as well, I am amazed that with the advent of cheaper transatlantic flights, the destination still remains on the periphery of the golfing map as a UK tourist destination for golfers.

The golf is supreme … Omni Championsgate Resort is less than five minutes away from my home and features two superb Greg Norman-designed courses and the David Leadbetter training school. Travelling from the airport to the villa on the toll road, you will see just before Kissimee Old Town, the famous Falcons Fire Course, another exceptional track. Every day, if you are visiting Disney, you will pass the Billion Dollar Ginn Reunion Resort with courses designed by Palmer, Nicklaus and Watson. It makes your mouth water simply driving through the estate. Disney has five outstanding tracks including the famous Magnolia were the Funai Classic is held in the fall. Within two hours is Golf's Hall of Fame, and the TPC at Sawgrass and TPC at Tampa are also all within two hours' driving. A golfer's dream, indeed there are over forty top-notch courses within twenty miles of where I live. So, when I needed to play the Americas in my five continent challenge, it was easy to decide where and when, the difficulty was finding the appropriate competitions.

My first visit to Florida had been in the spring of 1996. We had decided to take the family for a once-in-a-lifetime trip to Disneyland. I knew in June I needed to have a brain tumour removed; at best I would be deaf on my right side and at worst, well it did not bear thinking about. Again, I was fortunate and only lost my hearing at the end of a summer which saw endless complications and even catching meningitis at one stage. This time, I owed a considerable debt of gratitude to Professor Ramsden and the staff at Manchester Royal. If you wonder where your National Insurance Contributions have gone, I have had my fair share of benefit. As you may now be aware, I am a great proponent of our often-maligned National

Health Service. Whatever its failings, it was always there for me when I needed it most! Little did I realise it as we flew back over the Atlantic on my birthday, and everyone on the plane sang happy birthday to me, that I would often be back and indeed have a home in the sunshine state.

I played my first round of golf in Florida with my then ten-year-old son, Paul, on that first trip. We played a small nine hole executive course called The Polo. Superbly manicured, and set up as if it was a normal course, it was a

par thirty, I believe. You could hire all the equipment and in 1996 as I recall, I played with Callaways here for the first time. I pass this course often now and see that for $15 (about £8) you can still play a round – including the buggy hire. It is also where I later took the wife to play her first ever round in an attempt to get her interested. When I played with Paul, we were joined as a four ball by two Canadians, who were down for the winter. Both had been ill, one with a stroke ironically! Now they always came south for the warm weather from November to April, renting their homes back home to skiers. Half-way round, Paul hit a tee shot that dribbled off the fairway towards the water's edge. He marched down the bank and all I could see was his baseball hat over the ridge. Awaiting his shot, I heard a shriek, 'Daaad. Daaad.'

'What's up son' I replied. 'Look!' he waved his club angrily in the air. I walked over to him and saw on the edge of the water, his ball about ten inches away from a baby alligator of no more that six inches in length. 'It's only a baby. It can't hurt you, just whack the ball,' I muttered disdainly.

'But what about the mother' he said, pointing behind a bush at a large twelve-footer lolling in the sun looking menacingly at him, obviously concerned about her own offspring. I dropped a ball and said, 'Play this then' and marched away.

'What about my ball,' my son wailed, 'it's a Disney special with Goofy on.' The Rufty Tufty Canadian went to get it for him. Dad didn't!

My wife's first round there brought humour as well. Encouraging her to hit a six iron all the way round, she often berated me for not letting her use a wood. 'You want to keep them for yourself; you don't want me to win'. I think she enjoyed driving the buggy more than the golf. At one hole, a ninety-yard downhill to a green protected right and left by bunkers, I eventually felt she could do no damage with my five wood and might get a good roll downhill. She connected well and the ball rolled all the way down resting about four feet from the hole. 'See,' she says, 'it's easy with the proper clubs, you're unbelievable, trying to cheat me at golf!' With that, she jumped into the buggy and we set off downhill. In her excitement, she parked up in the left-hand bunker, walked straight through it and rapped her ball straight in, back to the buggy and drove straight off through the bunker to the next tee, leaving me with a big raking job.

As a resort, Orlando obviously offers all the magic of Disney – outstanding nightlife, great bars, restaurants and entertainment abound. I particularly love Epcot and can spend many an hour walking around the World Showcase. Where else can you walk through Canada, Britain into France, Morocco, China, America, Italy, Japan, Germany, Norway and Mexico? For me it is the

must-see in Orlando, but visitors should not just restrict themselves to the many distractions of Disney. Orlando is less than two hours from the outstanding beaches of the Atlantic, at Cocoa and Daytona and on the Gulf of Mexico at St Pete's and Clearwater. These compare to any in the world.

Again easily accessible is the historic town of St Augustine, the Greek fishing village of Tarpon Springs and the inland town of Mount Dora with all its olde-worldly charm and antiquity shops. A day out in Kissimee Old Town should be a priority too. Even kids will enjoy this cheap alternative. To miss out on these on a visit to Florida is akin to visiting Cornwall without going to St Ives, Polperro or the Eden Project.

Obviously for me, the golf was always going to be a big pull. When in 2004, Karen and I sold Riks, our sports bar in Wigan, she decided wisely that the proceeds needed reinvesting in property abroad, otherwise I would squander it. Wise decision. We had looked at Spain and been dismayed at what we could get for our money. Despite the flight-time (Karen's prime objection), I managed to persuade her to look at Florida after watching one of those property abroad shows. We went for a week, stayed in a travelodge and at the end of the week, acquired a four bed, three bath villa, with double garage, pool and spa for less than £120,000. It has since become a holiday home which has become self-sufficient as an investment and a home which I can now aspire to retire to and a base to warm my brittle bones in winter. Whilst the sub-prime market in the USA has certainly negated any capital growth, this was never a short-term issue for us. Compared with the problems of land grab in Spain, acquiring in Florida has been hassle-free, secure and very cheap. I would recommend any prospective buyer to take the plunge; I don't think you would regret it. We haven't for one moment.

Visiting two or three times a year, I decided to purchase a set of clubs to leave over there and therein lies another recommendation – any golfer should visit the huge discount stores on International Drive, particularly Edwin Watts, to see just what you can get for your money. I bought a full set of Callaway clubs, bag, trolley, shoes, etc. for less than £200. Subsequently, I bought a child's left-hand set for my little nephew, Freddie, for Christmas. The clubs and bag cost less at £30 than the £40 packaging to send them back home.

Playing golf in Florida is so easy and cheap. Every golf shop will have the Florida Golf Register with all course numbers, etc.; golfers should also keep their eyes open for the special offers. Every retail outlet will have discount booklets prominently on display free. Take them all. Discounts to restaurants, rides as well as golf are freely available and always accepted. Florida businesses run on these.

Since having the villa, it has opened up many opportunities for me to play some exceptional tracks. With our visitors, I have been able to play a round of golf, whilst the wife is happily enjoying herself at either one of the shopping malls that surround Orlando or just simply sunbathing by the pool. Most visitors' spouses prefer the malls of course where cheaper clothes in particular can be obtained leaving the guys a trouble-free day on the course. Only my mate, Steve, did not like this, for a man with such a big heart to have such a small wallet is irreconcilable. However, if his wife, Chris, and Karen were out shopping and he had a putt to win a hole, I would simply mention, Pierre Cardin or another prime store and the putt would slide past.

The first proper course I played in Florida was Falcons Fire, host of Open qualifiers in the past and a darned fine introduction into Floridian golf. On our first visit with Slasher Ken and Russ, we encountered the professional service you receive first-hand. Arriving at the club-house, we were met by two young chaps, the taller whom asked Russ for the keys. Russ passed them, believing he would get the bags out of the trunk but he got in the car and drove off down the hill with Russ in hot pursuit. The younger lad pointed out to Slasher he was taking the car to the buggies on which the bags would be placed and taken to the first tee ready for us, then the car would be parked up. Slasher let Russ run to the bottom of the hill and back again before telling him. It took Russ until the ninth to get his breath back and Slasher was four up then!

We encountered the number of tees prevalent in the USA courses for the first time; we attempted to play

The villa in Florida.

at the back of the five tee position, by the sixth we were back at the front. There are one or two memorable holes particularly the signature thirteenth. A par four dog-leg right over water, tempting the big hitter to cut the corner to a narrow fairway heavily protected by a ring of bunkers. A fine course (with buggy) for less that £40.

Subsequent to this, I have had the pleasure of playing a number of fine courses. I would particularly recommend the following, all coming in at less than £30 – Providence, Highlands Ridge and finally Ridgewood Lakes, which is a particular favourite of mine. These are all courses on house complexes where you play between the residences. They are always immaculately maintained. Another must-play course is the Trent Jones Public Course in the town of Celebration, rated the best public course in Florida. Celebration was Walt Disney's self-created town, which he designed and planned prior to his death. Think of Stepford Wives and you've got the picture. Again, this is somewhere the spouses can spend a day; pleasant shops, parks and you playing golf and meeting up in the evening at one of the town centre's exceptional restaurants. A magnificent day for all. Everyone who has visited the town loves it, except tight-arsed Skitty, because inevitably, his wife Chris buys loads of useless nick-nacks! The golf is again exceptional at about £40 as usual including buggy. Like most courses, they try to make up a four ball and when Skitty and I played, we partnered a husband and wife from Ohio. The round was memorable and as is always the case, featured a couple of unforgettable moments.

As lads, we have a few party tricks to adhere to; one is where a player drives and does not go past the lady's tee. On the eighth, Steve drove and it dribbled onto the ladies tee where the Ohian lady was waiting for us to complete our drives. Imagine her surprise as Steve immediately dropped his pants to his ankles and walked down to his ball and played the second with his trousers down. Once she had got over the shock of this, I had to explain our customary ritual. I can imagine the tales going around some Ohio golf clubs that summer. Steve had always had trouble with short chips so he had bought himself a chipper, one of those you use like a putter. The young lady was amazed with this club, she had never seen one and Steve, forever the gent, got great pleasure in teaching her how to use it and lent it to her on several holes. On the sixteenth, our match was evenly poised. He had never beaten me but was pushing me very close this day. I was just one up when he hit a smashing drive, and I followed suit. He hit his approach just short of the green; I hit a six iron to about twenty feet. He then shot off in his buggy back down the fairway and about five minutes later came back unbelievably distraught. 'Lost my chipper,' he says in tears. He takes his sand wedge and skulls the ball into the bunker, just as the Ohio lady walks across and hands him his chipper. His face was a picture, not helped when I holed my putt for a birdie three and he took three in the bunker, finishing with an eight and all but handing me the game.

Steve did however win the first trophy on my Florida Swing Tournament Run. I had decided to expand my five Continent challenges to include playing in amateur charity events as well in Florida; I was to play the Lakeland Aces Challenge in aid of Adult Retraining. This par three championship was to be held at the club at Eagle Brooke, a course used to holding Champions' Tour Events. I was also going to play with Steve in a pairs competition at Deer Creek, in the Davenport Charity Day for Cancer Research. I would complete the tri-challenge at Mystic Dunes in the Toys for Tots Open.

I can only say I had a marvellous time at all the events. They were all organised in exceptional style and competency – something I hope to bring to my events in future. All the courses were immaculately prepared for each event and I made some wonderful acquaintances. Indeed, that winter on my golfing sojourn, I played with Americans, Canadians, Swedes, Germans, Italians and Mexicans. There is something special about playing with a stranger whom you know you are unlikely to ever meet again. You neither pre-judge nor anticipate anything. You only wish each other the very best at all times, joined together for a short moment with a joint love of the game, playing just the elements and the course. A lot more diplomacy should be carried out on the golf course, I think.

The first competition I played in was in Lakeland at Eagle Brooke. What an event! On arriving we were

Karen at Hall of Fame.

given a brand spanking pair of Nike Golf Shoes and tee shirt, hat, balls, etc. The entrance fee had been $500 (about £260), so already I was starting to pull some back. The course, although a par seventy-two, was set up as eighteen par threes, each hole being from a position on the fairway where the pros in competition would approach from. It was a four-man scramble and I had been put in a sponsor's team. The greens are unbelievably slick. On the eighth, a contrived par three of 160 yards, I hit a five iron to twenty feet and being the only ball on the green, we chose mine and I holed the last of our four attempts for a birdie. We played consistently well, I birdied on my own, choosing my tee shot and I holed the putt at the twelfth. By the seventeenth we were four under, but at the seventeenth a normal par three 180 yard carry over water, no one hit the green and we had our only bogey. A par at the last saw us complete in fifty-one for second place in our category the sponsor's group. A great gala meal followed with some guests who starred in *Caddy Shack*, some of which had apparently been filmed here. The first part of my challenge had been completed and with some success.

The second competition was the Pairs at Deer Creek with Steve. Deer Creek is a small executive course par sixty, with twelve par threes and six par fours. Although small, it is as with all Florida courses, always in pristine condition. I have played it many times because I can get round in about two hours and be back home before Matron Karen notices I have gone. I really felt Steve and I would have a big chance here playing a better ball, for the level of competition was not particularly high and my accuracy allied with his safe putting, looked promising. On this day, we shot Steve's age, fifty-seven, never going to be good enough but for Steve something to talk about, for not many golfers shoot their age. We simply never holed a putt. However, Steve did take home a prize – it was the longest drive on the seventh. Steve and I drove about 240 but my ball had strayed off the fairway so could not count. Looking behind about a yard was the marker; Steve picked this up placed next to his ball and wrote 'S. SKITT'. At the prize-giving after, the organiser announces, 'Winner of the ladies longest drive – Ms S. Skitt'. It was the bloomin' ladies marker. All hell breaks loose as the women realised what had happened. One woman said, 'I should win, I was

only a foot behind.' Another claimed, 'But I was winning when he wrote his name on.' I thought Steve was going to be lynched. The organisers appeased the unfortunate ladies with half a dozen balls each. I was disappointed they would not let Steve keep the trophy but they can't take the title off him of 'Ladies Big Hitter'!

The final part of the tri-challenge was the 'Toys for Tots' event at Mystic Dunes. Now if you can only play one course in Orlando then this has to be it. A super challenge made even more incredible by the quality and difficulty of the greens. I have read since that the greens were rated second only to Augusta and better than Cypress Point, Pinehurst and Pebble Beach; they really

Ian with the 'Toys for Tots' Trophy.

are that good. This was to be my competitive highlight in Florida as we finished second in the whole competition partly thanks to my birdie at the last. Another unbelievably organised day and a trophy to boot, what more could I ask for. Ten months previously, I could not walk, but now I was walking away from this prestigious course with a trophy. Naturally, I was ecstatic.

For visitors interested in playing in local events, you will be made warmly welcome. Buy Wednesday evening's *Ledger* paper, as it always has a golf supplement listing all the forthcoming competitions and always has plenty of discounted course vouchers as well.

Karen relaxes at St Augustine.

After Steve and Chris left, I confirmed with Karen she felt comfortable enough with my health to finalise the trip to Australasia, and on receiving Matron's 'OK', I spent the last two weeks in Florida doing some serious practice. I played in the evening at the stunning par three floodlit, Palmer-designed Legends' Walk at Orange Lakes.

A fine challenge was made better by the experience of night play. I also played Championsgate, both the National and International, for the first time. The International had hosted the parent and child competition the previous week, with luminaries such as Nicklaus, Palmer, Norman, Trevino, Singh, Nelson, Duval, and Langer all playing with their offspring, so the course was in exceptional condition. Whilst I preferred Mystic Dunes, there is not much in it; Championsgate is a superb golf facility. I liked the National slightly more than the much more illustrious International. Both are formidable challenges – no wonder Norman and Leadbetter are associated with it. You do pay for what you get however. A round here and at the Dunes is usually three figures in American terms, but still probably only about £65 UK money, great value compared to back here, but relatively expensive when compared to other Floridian courses.

Finally, any keen golfer should at some stage in Florida head up to St Augustine and the Hall of Fame. Play the simulators, feel close to greatness with the players' mementos. Have pictures with the replica trophies, and see the actual American trophies. Again, this is probably only for the very keen, but Karen enjoyed it – especially the simulators and putting green.

In Orlando, especially around International Drive, one can complete the Floridian golf experience by playing one of the splendid miniature or crazy golf courses that abound. Feed the crocs, explode the volcano. With vouchers, this experience (and it is one) can be unbelievably cheap. Ensure you win though, for to be de-throned as family champ can be very embar-rassing.

The stay at the villa certainly meant a lot to me – two visits were cancelled because of my illness.

Ian with the 'Ladies Driving Champ'..

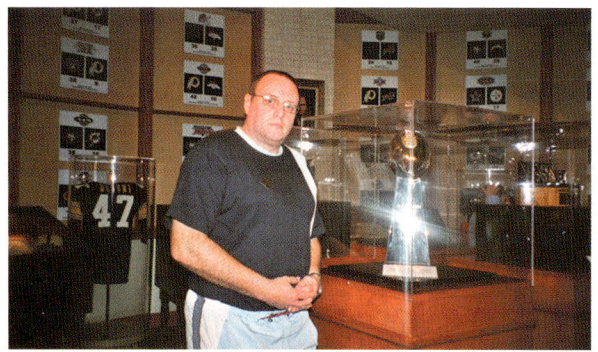 

The sun had improved my general well-being immensely. I felt up to Australia and Karen herself looked better than ever. We had enjoyed visits from the Skitts and the in-laws, it certainly has focused my mind on business matters as this is how I now intend to spend my retirement. Whilst the Skitts, Steve and Chris, were with us, I gave Chris a nickname which has stuck since, 'Echo'. Every morning Karen's first words to me are 'have you had your tablets, had some breakfast', every bloomin' morning! For a fortnight in Florida, I got it in stereo!

Even Steve can't clear this.

10. Australia

Magnificent Melbourne

The planning of a trip down-under, I was about to find out, was substantially different from a little jaunt across Europe, across the pond to America, or even 'the long way down to South Africa' as Ewan Macgregor so vividly described his trip to Cape Town by motorbike. The sheer magnitude of the world comes into play when you start to look at distances, time in the air, hours in front, etc. No wonder it's called the 'Land Down Under'. I had managed to persuade Matron I was fit for this trip but when I considered a twenty-three-hour journey, I was slightly apprehensive. I tried always to fit in a stop both going out and coming back, but that would take more time than the three weeks I had allocated to be away from work. So compromises had to be made.

When planning the Australian Tour, the main golf championship being in Hobart, the wife had made it clear she wanted to visit and spend some time in Sydney on the way back. Then I had to identify a stopover on the way out. To be honest, I chose Melbourne not because I knew anything about the place but quite simply because it is a sporting mega city. The golf courses were rated amongst the best, naturally a big plus to a social golfer like me. Their rugby league and soccer teams had won the national titles. It's the home of the Australian Tennis Open and Formula One Grand Prix and of course, horse racing's Melbourne Cup and the famous Melbourne Cricket Ground.

So, with that in mind, the outward trip sorted itself out. Manchester to London, London to Hong Kong, two-hour changeover, Hong Kong to Melbourne. Four days in this sporting metropolis at the time of the Australian Tennis Open – great timing. Then to Tasmania for the competition, a week in Hobart, back to Sydney for five days, home the same way but a last weekend in Hong Kong, culminating with playing golf in Asia, completing my five continent challenge. I spent hours trawling the internet for the best options. In the end, I let James at Travelbag sort it out for me – a supremely efficient service that I have since used many times. His details are in the Ac-knowledgements. He immediately asked had I considered upgrading, was I flexible within a few days of flying, and by doing this, he got us an exceptional first-class deal on Cathay Pacific. Economy was about £580, upgraded to £3,800. Now I appreciate most social golfers could not consider this, but as my mate, Bernard, says if you are the best damned social golfer, then you should travel this way! Bet Tiger doesn't go economy! If you can afford it, it is worth every penny.

The outward trip from London to Hong

Kong starts in the first-class lounge at Heathrow, then gets better. We travelled on one of Cathay Pacific's newer planes with the modernised first-class cabin, which was a lounge at the front of the plane with only six compartments, each turned into a bed. You had a twenty-inch TV screen, own wardrobe, were provided with pyjamas, toilet and a shower, and we were the only occupants waited on hand and foot by two stunning oriental ladies. I found out on this flight that Matron does not like caviar so I had hers, free choice of wine, à la carte menu cooked on the plane when you want it. An in-flight entertainment system that put all the Sky packages to shame. What a way to travel! I had been apprehensive, I thought if something does happen where will we be, and watched the map showing our current position periodically – Denmark, Latvia, Poland, Russia, can't be ill now, don't want to put down here, by the time we were over the fourth or fifth something – Stan, I could not give a monkeys – my bed was made up, I was well-fed and watered, well-wined and slept until we approached Hong Kong, woken by the smell of cooking bacon.

The older oriental lady (one would have been in her 20s, the other in her 40s), tapped me on the shoulder half-way through the flight and said, 'I remember you from the '80s, Mr Halliwell, and you have not changed a bit.' Now unless she worked at the *Pacific Ocean* or *Happy Palace* in Wigan's town centre, I fail to see how she could have! However, it made my day. I had a perm in those days and was often mistaken for Tom Selleck. Still, it tickled Matron, boosted my already inflated ego and I went to sleep practising my winning speech at the Wrest Point Masters. Travelling like this, about to play Royal Melbourne, it was in the bag! No-one will be better prepared than me. As I was to find out, a bit of talent was still required.

When we arrived in Hong Kong, I was very disappointed because it was wet and misty (portents of what was to come), and I had eagerly anticipated that much-filmed landing between all the skyscrapers. My oriental admirer sensing my disappointment pointed out that, 'it's a new airport, Mr Halliwell, on Landau Island, you don't fly through the city like you did last time you were here.' Matron now thinks I have a secret life.

The flight to Melbourne was on an older plane with the cabin at the front where they make all the economy passengers walk through to see what they are missing. Once again, the service was impressive, immaculate and made the nine-hour flight pass so very quickly. We arrived in Melbourne at 9 p.m. their time after some twenty-three hours in the air, but totally refreshed and ready for our adventure. For the first time in twelve months a flight had not stressed me and it was a good job. As we waited for our luggage, Karen's name was called over the tannoy – her case was in London, but more importantly, my clubs were somewhere! After I had a little tantrum, there was nothing we could do but head for the hotel and accept that Cathay Pacific would get them to us as a matter of urgency. I could replace

First Class opulence.

River Yarra, Melbourne.

Matron's clothes, but not my clubs! This wouldn't happen to Tiger. Must ask James if there is a super first-class service!

I am not sure what I expected from Melbourne but I had certainly not expected to be taken in by the simple beauty of the city. A city is just a city, and if you have seen one you've seen them all. However, Melbourne was to prove to be the perfect base for a social golf tour, particularly if the wife is tagging along. We stayed at the Saville on Russell Street; this was relatively inexpensive by Melbourne standards. It is bang in the centre of China Town and ten minutes' walk from all major attractions. The location was ideal. The rooms had a kitchenette, lounge and separate bedroom and whilst not expensively decorated, were clean and well-maintained. There were no complaints. The hotel had a pool, gym and a patio deck to sort a nice tan out. The only negative was that the bar closed at eleven, but in a city that never sleeps that was only a small inconvenience.

The city must have come a long way since Hollywood '50s diva and actress, Ava Gardner (star of the 1959 film *On the Beach* which was filmed in Melbourne), said the city was the perfect place to make a film about the end of the world. I could relate more to a previous comment made over 140 years ago – in the 1860s, George Augustus Sala, a British journalist, had described Melbourne in London's *Daily Telegraph* in even more glowing terms: 'I found Melbourne a really astonishing city with broad streets full of handsome shops and crowded with bustling well-dressed people.' He dubbed the city 'Marvellous Melbourne', saying it was 'teeming with wealth and humanity'.

That first night, we found the obligatory English pub, the *Elephant and Barrow* – it took me four days to realise what was in the barrow! We ate in a local Chinese where the meal was gorgeous and so cheap. Pick any of the smells and aromas of China Town and they're unique – you feel hungry from the moment you leave the hotel. In the pub, Karen first noticed the dress style of the women, even the younger ones; you notice first of all that there are not many overweight people in this city, but despite having bodies to die for, the citizens, male and female, all dressed very conservatively. Melbourne certainly seems to have adopted a more conservative character than its sister city, Sydney. While Melbourne turned towards subtle

European styles, Sydney took on a racier, American feel. Having now visited both I believe this still applies today, with residents agreeing that 'Sydney-siders will throw a party while Melbournians will give a dinner party'. Perhaps this is also why Melbourne residents are known for wearing black, the colour of laid-back bohemian chic. When making interstate visits, Melbournians are accused of dressing too often in 'Melbourne black'. But it is a tag they are happy to wear. They wouldn't dream of wearing the garish colours seen on the streets of Sydney or on the beaches of Queensland. Like in most large cities, there seems to be a large gay and lesbian community that is often found near the oriental areas. Perhaps they feel less threatened there? In the *Elephant,* one attractive Amazonian-type woman oblivious that I was with Karen, took a shine to the wife and simply approached her at the bar and told her she was beautiful. She was right of course, but that would not happen in Wigan.

The next day, oriental efficiency lived up to expectations and the clubs and the case arrived undamaged as promised. We decided to go to the beach – it was a lovely hot day, so hot that the tennis stars down at Geelong, refused to play. The best beach in Melbourne to visit has to be St Kilda. Melbourne has a super tram system which takes you to all parts of the city. Tickets can be bought in virtually every shop and it's the easiest way to get round.

St Kilda is enjoying a resurgence in popularity, and it's not hard to see why. With its picturesque bay-side setting, its proximity to Melbourne and its beaches, restaurants and café lifestyle, it makes a pleasant

change from the busy city. St Kilda used to be best-known for drugs and prostitution, integral to the area since the 1940s when American servicemen lived here. The prostitutes and drug addicts have largely been pushed out by the rapidly rising cost of real estate, and St Kilda is now more reminiscent of its heyday in the first half of the twentieth century when it was a fashionable suburb.

Near the pier are the St Kilda Sea Baths, part of the Melbourne community since the 1850s and now newly-restored. Mixed bathing, long a controversial practice, came to be accepted in the area around 1910. Now this quintessentially urban beach is a weekend mecca for visitors and locals, from cyclists and rollerbladers to windsurfers and kiteboarders. It is usually easy to pick the Australians from the foreigners: the Aussies are the ones sitting in the shade, with a broad hat, sunglasses and covered in sunscreen while the rest of us are baking in the sun.

We had a wonderful day and spent the evening down at the sensational Federation Complex on the banks of the Yarra. This really is an architectural inspiration – bars, restaurants, open-air theatre, and museums. It shows just what can be achieved in the modern era. UK planners, take a look at this development.

Today, Melbourne is believed to be the third largest Greek city (after Athens and Thessaloniki); is said to have more Maltese (second and third generation) than Malta itself, and large Italian and south-east Asian populations. The 1980s saw Melbourne accept and embrace these immigrants and all they brought with them – most of all their food. Melbourne is the food capital of Australia. Old Australian cuisine has been brought up-to-date with a fusion of Asian and Western ingredients to create 'Modern Australian' cuisine. The eclecticism, allied to the Australian readiness to experiment with new tastes and food combinations, has transformed Melbourne cooking.

The city has more than its share of outstanding restaurants and down by the river and on Collins Street are some outstandingly chic wine bars often frequented by the Melbourne establishment.

After my day at the golf, we spent our final day walking down by the Yarra and a splendid stroll it was too, past the Rod Laver arena where the Fed Express was to be derailed later that week in the Australian Open, saw Andy Murray disconsolate after his first round exit in the Aussie Open, carried on to the magnificent MCG. Any sporting buff will know that this place oozes history.

That last evening, we went down to the newer development by the dockland which is still being developed. This will, I believe, be a fine addition to enhance the experience of visiting 'Magnificent Melbourne'.

Melbourne is a changing city, its nineteenth century architectural heritage is complemented by dynamic new buildings and a renewed confidence in the future. With its sporting heritage and golf courses of exceptional quality, it's a social golfer's delight.

When I knew we were stopping over in Melbourne on the way to Hobart, I was aware that this wonderful city is the epicentre of Australian golf. Indeed, the state of Victoria has produced some of the

world's finest golfers, five-times Open Champion, Peter Thomson, and the legend, Greg Norman, for starters. Indeed that summer, the European PGA had been in town with the Australian Masters at Huntingdale whilst the Women's Open was to be held at Kingston Heath.

Quality courses abound, but if you have the opportunity you have to play the 'Daddy of them all', the world-ranked Royal Melbourne. In any rankings, the Royal appears in the top ten and is consistently ranked number one in Australia. When reading up on the club, the superlatives abound …

It burns me up that with all the billions of dollars spent on course construction over the past 50 years, all the architects together have been unable to build another Royal Melbourne.
Gene Sarazen

Royal Melbourne is one of the classic golf courses of the world. Its very Augusta-ish. We all have our preferences where we rank them, but Royal Melbourne is one of the greats.
Nick Faldo

The tour won't putt on better greens than those all year. The course is a 2nd shot course like Augusta, but this is a lot tougher.
Ernie Els

It is hard to imagine that the game of golf gets any better than Royal Melbourne. To all, from the purist, weekend hacker and professional, it remains the absolute embodiment of golfing perfection – if indeed such a thing exists.
Planet Golf

I was amazed how easy it was, compared with the UK, to get to play the course. A phone call and faxed letter of introduction and that was it …Thursday 9 a.m., West Course: and off I went.

The first thing that hit me was the location, not on the seafront more on heath land surrounded by urban developments, a less likely place for such an historic and talked-about course than I had ever imagined. This area of old grazing land was the home of some of the best golfing real estate in the world however.

On entering the complex, you immediately see the impressive old colonial club-house, no doubt significantly added to over the years. On the left of this are the newer pro shop and changing rooms. I was early so sat outside on a park bench. Despite being inland, the wind was already getting up similar to what one would expect on a links at home: clearly this course would have hidden teeth. A polite old gent (in his 70s, I would guess), introduced himself in best Aussie drawl, 'Guest from the UK are you sir? Welcome to our club. Waiting for Reception? Come on in, I'll show you round.'

He then gave me a comprehensive tour of the club's memorabilia, history and walked me through the hallowed ranks of the board-room, adorned with pictures of Australia's greats – Thomson, Nagle, Marsh, Graham, Elkington to Norman and Ogilvy. I was informed that every Australian major winner had a photo here somewhere. Norman's driver from the '80s was also on show. How prehistoric that looked now, yet couldn't he still whack it back then. I must admit it may not be every golfer's cup of tea, but I was mesmerised and it was a perfect introduction to this wonderful arena of golfing history and accomplishment.

I went to reception to pay my $300 Aus (about £140), which sounds a lot but compare that with home. The young lady was exquisite, giving me a promotional brochure for the club, a set of three embossed Royal Melbourne balls, cards and maps for both East and West Courses and I then proceeded to the pro shop to pick up my regulatory hat and polo shirt for posterity and my caddy I had booked for a further $150.

Hole Three, Royal Melbourne.

Royal Melbourne, like most established courses at the turn of the twentieth century, is not equipped for today's modern electronic cart – the placement of bunkers, layout of holes and run in to green make them a total impracticality. So, I have found on my travels, let someone else take the strain, plus if you are solo playing, they are at worst still good company with a few tales to tell, and at best, they provide essential knowledge in respect of course and particularly green knowledge. My caddy was a young assistant pro called Dave, twenty-two-years-old playing off four. I must admit I felt a bit intimidated in his presence as I had expected a much older partner, not a young brash Aussie who could probably thump the ball 300 yards or more. Furthermore, I was surprised when he placed my clubs straight onto a trolley, clearly this was one caddy who did not believe in humping my oversized bag around.

I had decided to play the West Course not the East for two reasons – every book described MacKenzie's West as the superior course to his apprentice Russell's East course. Much more important was that the composite course which is the championship one set up at the Royal and the one Tiger will be playing in the 2011 Presidents Cup, has twelve holes in the West and just six from the East. Now I must advise at this point that anyone playing the Royal should leave two days free and play both, because having now returned to the UK, I feel there's a void I should have filled.

Walking to the first tee, Dave and I exchanged pleasantries. Coming from Wigan, sport was always an easy icebreaker. Soccer or rugby and the Open at Birkdale were easy ways of ensuring a discourse. Dave had been told Melbourne was similar to Birkdale and would be interested in my views later. The first hole heads away from the club house and is a 392 metres (431 yards) par four index eight – I get a stroke! I notice that the first hole is in the composite at number seventeen so I quickly realise that both courses are very intertwined as I play this hole aiming for what I later find out to be the seventeenth on the East. Taking my driver and armed with the knowledge I must stay left, I swing my first drive with no anticipation or expectation of anything. Most social golfers enjoy their pre-game warm up courtesy of the nineteenth hole and that first swing and first hole

Hole Twelve, Royal Melbourne.

Hole Seven, Royal Melbourne.

is always in my mind a *Stingray* moment, from the '60s puppet show, 'anything can happen in the next five minutes.' Remarkably, this drive flew relatively off the middle well left – I was aiming down the wrong fairway but about my usual 240 yards. 'Super shot', my new friend advised, 'Prime position, A1 well done – great first shot at the Royal, not many can say that.'

I thought I won't shatter his illusions – I was about 200 yards from the green, confirmed by Dave in the 180 metres he paced off from the 200 metres. I remember and am grateful to my old mate, Johnny Chapman, who on my first visit to Tunisia taught me how to quickly change metres to yards. 'Divide by ten and add on,' seems simple now but I've lost count of the times I have passed on that knowledge and acted like the Pythagoros of the golf course.

'Five iron,' Dave chirped up, so I quickly had to advise on my lack of beef, blaming my stroke for the lack of distance without telling him I had never been able to hit a five iron much further than 160 yards. Still, it got his sympathy and explained why a six-foot, fifteen-stone muppet could not hit the ball very far. He offered me my three wood. I went down to a five wood, far too early to use the three with my swing. Another good connection, off the middle, straight at the flag, aside of that other green, not sure what that is: leaving a wedge of about forty yards or so I thought.

'Fantastic, great course management, chip and a putt for a par,' Dave boomed. Now I am all for optimistic encouragement but this appeared over the top.

'How do you see this?' he says. Full sand or half-wedge I am thinking.

'Over here, too many players use a lob wedge and try for perfection but I think you're a seven iron pitch and run man coming from the UK.' Then it dawned on me, my ball was only just off the first green, the one I had been trying to play away from on both previous shots. I was four yards off the green, pin five on, nothing in between, so I would always use my six and simply punch on aka a putt. It was a shot I had played numerous times at home aiming for the dustbin lid, and this one was straight at the flag. For a moment, I thought it might drop but at the last moment it broke sharp right and trundled seven-feet past downhill. My caddy was distraught, 'My fault, I should have told you to play well above the pin, sorry won't happen again.' Looking at my par putt, on taking the flag away, Dave confidently stated, 'Two balls outside right edge, Ian' and I took aim, I hit the ball exactly where instructed but back uphill, under-hit it and the break kicked in early and the ball lipped out. Tap in for bogey, par with my stroke, two Stableford points, no worries, no disgrace, did not look a prat and no-one knows what really went on.

The second at the West is actually the tenth on the composite, and the third through the sixth are the first four on the championship course, so I knew I was now about to play some major golfing terrain. On the second tee, I got the dreaded nod from the fairway to play through, four members clearly assuming I must be a somebody and wanted me out of the way. All golfers will at some time have been called through and then proceeded to hit a duffer which does not even reach the poorest shot of the group in front. It is always my dread when asked to play through. The second is a par five, 439 metres (479 yards), stroke index one, no shot. Although since my stroke, my competitive handicap is seventeen, I still try and score to my pre-stroke handicap of eleven. I surveyed the fairway, one of the group was in the bushes some hundred yards from the tee, another in the back of the large cavernous bunker that ran for seventy yards alongside the right edge of the fairway. The other two were central about twenty-two yards, my A1 shot distance. I swung hard and connected well. I knew I had cleared the two longer shots but as can happen when you try and cream the ball, I brought in a late fade which sent it into the front of the bunker at about 240, but I was in front of the members. I ignored Dave's advise to risk my five wood, having got in front of them, I was not about to leave my ball in the sand and hit a comfy eight iron into the middle of the fairway, now about 160 from the green all up hill. I decided to hit my five wood. Another nice connection saw the ball dribble onto the front of the green. A birdie putt to six-inches, easy tap in for my first par at the Royal. Dave was overjoyed and really impressed with my course management. 'Can't teach that,' he says 'wish we could, knowing your limitations is such a major aspect of this game.' Being lucky I thought, but I'm not about to burst his bubble. Reading later, I find out Lee Trevino in 1974 at the height of his powers took a nine here but in '85, Greg Norman eagled it to win the Australian Open. Tex Mex eat your hat, my five more akin to Greg. Tiger, Phil, Vijay, I will be watching carefully in 2011!

On the third tee, I realised the next four holes were as close as I would get to playing a run of holes as in the composite and I was not disappointed. Individually three, four, five and six at the West are fine holes in their own right but as a stretch of four holes, they are as good as anything I have ever played and as a starting four they would be imperious. The third is a dog-leg left, with a large bunker on the right to stop you opening up the fairway. At only 360 yards, it is now an easy birdie opportunity for the pros who would I assume cut off the corner, but heavily sloping and well protected by three bunkers green will, I am sure, still protect the card somewhat. I took five courtesy of playing into the left-hand trap. Using the social golfer's adage of 'just get out', which I did, a twenty-foot par putt was too much to ask for and at stroke index twelve, I dropped my first shot. The fourth is a 470-yards par five, again the

Hole Six, Royal Melbourne.

pros would deem this a major opportunity. They would simply drive over the fairway bunkers and hit a mid-iron approach to a raised green again, taking out of play the protecting bunkers. I played perfectly routinely. Solid drive, centre fairway position, fivewood lay up again fortunately avoiding the bunkers. Heeding advice to wedge to below the flag, I left an eighteen footer for birdie, never in with a chance however, three foot tap in for par. Second par at the opening pair of par fives, clearly identifying where on the composite a good score must come from. The fifth is the first par three. Now this is where I differ from my much-travelled friends at *Planet Golf*. They describe the set of four par threes here as some of the best in the world. True, they all have great greens, superb bunkers and have differing lengths and would play to differing wind strengths as they all run in different directions. However, I like my threes to be visually stunning when I stand on the tee. None here were, and that's part of the problem about not being able to see the sea anywhere on the course. At 176 yards, I decided to hit my rescue, because it was so heavily protected, and this would give me an opportunity to run this up through the entrance to the green. I could not have hit it better and the ball ran straight up to finish about twenty feet pin high left of the cup.

'Interesting putt,' Dave commented, 'you really need to be right of the flag here. Sorry should have told you.' Right of flag, I just aim for the green, silly boy, I can miss putts from anywhere. I soon realised what he meant, for the green plateaued out to the right, and I was on the top of a slope putting down at least a ten-foot incline.

'Gentle now, right lip,' was the only advice offered and not very confidently at that. I stroked the ball and it passed the right lip by a millimetre then hurtled twelve feet past. In sheer frustration, I marched up to the ball and rapped it back and much to my surprise, it dropped for a par three.

'Told you, much easier putt from the right,' Dave said and it took a lot of restraint not to shove my putter where the sun don't shine – I got a three man, five holes three pars, two over – I was delighted.

The sixth has been deemed to be one of the world's best of the championship tees, the hole often described as a strategic masterpiece. Tiger's tee was perched high above where I was playing from. A ninety-degree dog-leg right, which all golfers would be tempted to bite off more than can be chewed and so was I. I hit a driver with a fade which I confidently expected to leave an easy approach. However, I was a bit tight and ran off the fairway into some light sandy scrub making the approach much more difficult. The view to the sixth is one of Mackenzie's most photographed. From the fairway, there is a gentle slope up to the green set in a natural amphitheatre, that is guarded by a massive deep trap on the left side. The green's last defence is its putting surface, which slopes in many directions and can turn almost the length of the putt.

In 1987, in the Australian Open, it provoked a walk-out by the professionals when Sandy Lyle and Greg Norman complained a pin position to be completely unfair. The upshot was that the final round was postponed for a day. 'Soft sods', can't have played Mystic Hills in Orlando! Despite the truly horrendous pin position I encountered, I left with a five net four, stroke index was two, my tee shot costing me dear. The seventh at the west, eleventh on composite, is an uphill par three, to the highest part of the terrain. Playing 150 yards to a virtually totally protected green, there is no room for error. I took a five iron, more in hope than in anticipation and gave it 100%, ensuring I got the ball well airborne. Clearing the front bunker, I had clearly hit the green, expecting a comment from Dave (but receiving no more than an acknowledgement by way of appreciative grunt), I climbed uphill and for the first time, got a magnificent view of both courses. On competition days, I would assume with the crowds, sponsors' tents, etc., it would be quite majestic. I had left a sixteen-footer for my first birdie, looked pretty straight, 'inside left.' Dave proffered his regulatory opinion. In truth, this was to be the best chance I had, but I aimed slightly outside the left lip and that's where it stayed rolling three inches past but despite my disappointment, three successive pars, five in total just two over. Not bad for a cripple!

Hole Five, Royal Melbourne.

The eighth and ninth are not on the composite and maybe my intensity levels fell, or perhaps normal service resumed. Two par fours, the eighth 380 yards, the ninth 420 yards were both bogeyed, leaving me forty at the turn, playing off eleven, twenty Stableford points – very respectable. It's not that either hole was poor, it's just that in the context of the course, they failed to stand out. Bunkers cost me dear, I missed my first fairway for a while at nine, driving into the right hand bunkers that split the eighth and ninth fairway and on the eighth when my approach finished short in the green side trap.

The tenth, eleventh and twelfth form twelve to fourteen on the composite and again were quite remarkable, memorable and outstanding. The tenth is a truly delightful hole. Only just over 300 yards so eminently reachable by Tiger and his pals yet any birdie earned here will be hard-earned. The sporting length of this hole offers the ultimate temptation to drive for the hole and possible eagle but to get there means clearing an enormous chasm of a bunker and you would feel very small if you ended up in there. The green is perched on top of a crest of the hill and anything less than the perfect shot will roll aimlessly away leaving a treacherous pitch back. A sloping very quick green then awaits. For me, the line was definitely right and then a pitch on, but the fairway slopes right encouraging any over-hit shots to the scrub and trees bordering the right hand side. I over-hit and my approach out of light scrub got a flyer over the back, chip back and two putts. 300 yards and no shot – were the wheels coming off?

The eleventh is a 455 yards substantial par four which dog-legs to the left and to a green of substantial undulations. These are bad distances for me, despite a sound drive of about 240 and well hit five wood, I could not reach the green and had to chip over the bunker and two putt again. In truth it was a par five for me and marked as stroke

Hole Thirteen, Royal Melbourne.

one on the card; I could see why – a five was my best effort. The twelfth offers the alternate option. A par five for me but I understand par four for Tiger; it was 480 yards, key to avoid the many traps, which I do and complete an easy par to succesfully par all three par fives so far. Thirteen through to seventeen, again play no part in the composite as they are across the road in a separate paddock. Despite that, I found these to be a very pleasant quartet of holes. Thirteen being a par three just under 150 yards, again well-protected by bunkers which I unnervingly found and regulation out and two putts followed. The fourteenth leads to the extremity of the course. At 380 yards, this played as a drive to a wide fairway and seven iron approach to a well-guarded green and a thirty-foot two putt for nice par, back on track. The fifteenth was the last of the par fives and remarkably similar to the others it was – about 480 yards, solid drive, five wood and wedge, two putts, fourth par on the par fives. I suspect that in itself hides the weakness of the course in this modern age. The sixteenth is the last of the par threes at 220 yards and surrounded by cavernous bunkers that preclude a run-up. It epitomises all I hate about par threes. I used my driver to hopefully get enough height to stop the ball. Bunkered, I played my one and only good sand shot of the day to two foot, but I'd had plenty of practice, I felt like Rommel. Easy putt which sank on the third rotation round the lip for another par.

The last two, holes seventeen and eighteen, play as fifteen and sixteen on the composite and again in anyone's language, represent a super finish. The seventeenth at 440 yards. At 250 yards, the fairway drops into a valley and rises again revealing the green as a spectacular target. I had not three putted all round so was due one and here it came for a bogey five. I needed a birdie at the last to break eighty; I had hardly looked like getting one all day, so set my stall on a par for an eighty and thirty-nine Stableford points. The drive is over a hill with plenty of bunkers and then sharp dog-leg left. I hit my longest and best drive of the day, 270 plus with a fade. I was left with about 160 yards and hitting my trusty five iron to front edge, leaving a twenty footer for birdie. In my dreams that would have rolled in but on a day when I lagged the ball well. Again, the dustbin lid approach, dead length easy tap in for a four.

In truth like many historic courses, the Royal is succumbing to today's advances in technology but also, I do believe, in the increased athleticism of today's modern golfer. Kiwi and former US Open Champion, Michael Campbell, remarked that from 1996 to 2002, he noticed from his yardage books, he was twenty yards further. However, despite this, the course record is still only sixty-three by Open Winner, Ian Baker Finch, in 1990.

This brings me back to Birkdale, the terrain and hole design is akin to that great seaside links in my own north west and anyone who can shoot sixty-three at the Royal must have a chance at Birkdale, as was proved when Finch followed this up with his Open victory. The five easily reached par fives ensure that the defence of this course to the pros has to be pin placement and green speed and penal rough in specific places.

The Royal is so special because it embodies so many of Mackenzies abiding principles:

- it is arranged so that the low handicapper or absolute beginner should be able to enjoy the round irrespective of the score;

- the course should be in beautiful surroundings;

- sufficient number of heroic carries from the tee but alternative strategic options for the weaker player;

- infinite variety of strokes required;

- complete absence of the annoyance and irritation of searching for lost balls.

Hole Seventeen, Royal Melbourne.

Rarely have I concluded a round feeling less tired and so elated. Truly the social golfer's heaven.

I did not lose a ball, scored well but in truth left nothing on the course. I would have had to hole some stunning putts to go much lower. I spent a little time after the round discussing my game with Dave, who had nothing but complimentary comments and whose only big criticism was my safety first on the greens, however readily agreeing this could have led to three putts.

Eighty at Royal Melbourne, bring Hobart on, I had no fears. Little did I know what the golfing demons had in store for me.

Hobart

Hobart is a three quarters of an hour flight from Melbourne over the length of Tasmania, situated at the far south of the island. From the air, Tasmania is a barren, yet lush island which was suffering from lack of rain as could be seen with the large numbers of burned areas caused by forest fires that were rife that summer. The airport is about ten miles from the centre of Hobart, across the magnificent Hobart Bridge that spans the river separating central and southern Hobart from the northern suburbs. It is obvious as you

cross the bridge that this natural harbour, similar to that at Sydney, that dictated the whereabouts of the settlements in those early years. The many small boats in the harbour mingle with industrialised cargo ships and large ocean cruise liners.

We arrived at Wrest Point Casino, about three miles out of the centre, right on the coast at Wrest Point, named because of the large duck colony that apparently has resided here and still does in the grounds since (and before) the Brits arrived three centuries ago.

The Casino is magnificently placed overlooking the entire harbour. Our room in the tower was

Ian at Hobart Harbour.

sensational and the views down to the bridge were awesome. I recall that one Sunday in the 1970s, an oil tanker ran into the bridge and brought it down, killing about twenty or so. If it had been a week-day, hundreds would have perished.

The Casino has three excellent restaurants. The revolving one on the top of the tower offers a complete panoramic view of Hobart which is sensational and should not be missed. Karen's motion sickness reared its head here and she did not particularly enjoy the meal or view, but I did. We both agree however that the Pier 1 restaurant, on the pier naturally, was best value for food in the resort. Every evening, there was always entertainment by way of very competent local singers in the cocktail bar. In the sports bar, there was a happy hour between seven and eight, where all golfers told tales of fisherman proportions. Then there was the casino. All round the resort was the perfect base for a golf trip.

We were a ten-minute bus ride from Hobart, or as Karen found whilst I was golfing, a thirty-minute walk along the coast. Hobart has a feel of Cornwall, or even Gibraltar, with old Victorian buildings everywhere. The history of the island is everywhere, the names of all the original prisoners and their gaolers recorded for posterity as if they were royalty. Indeed they are feted as such here.

I particularly liked the Salamanca Square area, on the harbour front. Based without doubt on Macintosh Square in Gibraltar, this is a wonderful place to spend an evening. Colourful art galleries mingle with wine bars and restaurants from around the world. Every culinary requirement could be found within this half-mile radius. We had Greek, Spanish tapas, Italian, Indian, seafood and steaks in our week here. Without exception, every meal was outstanding and great value.

As a major port, a lot of trips naturally can be made by boat. If Karen had sea legs, it would have opened up a considerable range of excursions as the cruises were extremely cheap. Friends recommended the day trip to Tahune Forest where you can walk through the treetops along a forty-metre high steel air walk. This 671 metres walk takes you through the canopy of some of Tasmania's famous trees, including celery top pine, sassafras, myrtle and blackwood and towering gigantic stringy barks. It offers majestic views of the Huon and Picton rivers.

The town of Clarence, not far from Tasmania Golf Club, is also worth a visit. It has probably the best beaches in Tasmania and is handily placed to visit the vineyards of Coal River Valley or the majestic historic manor house at Richmond.

Hobart City is a pleasant, clean and tidy city. Easy to walk round, nice tea shops and some fine shops.

Salamanca Square.

I had my hair cut in Hobart – trying anything to improve my golf. The hairdresser was a lady in her mid-40s, I would think, who hailed from Hull, had left the UK in 1976, never to return. She had moved here from Sydney and was now contemplating retiring to France. She bemoaned the lack of a social life in Hobart – there are no concerts, films arrive years after anywhere else, little culture, so she felt she lived in a backwater, begrudgingly accepting it was a hell of an attractive one at that. She acknowledged that it was a fine place to visit, but a week here is enough she said, and it probably is.

Tasmanians are warm, friendly islanders, Australian through and through but still have more in common with the English than the mainlanders who do treat them as backwoods-people.

I should have hired a car and then been able to see more of the island, maybe next time …

The Wrest Point Masters, Australia's most prestigious amateur golf event which was the main reason for my visit; the competition I missed last year due to my stroke – the main impetus behind every press-up, every gym session, every massage. All the pain I put myself through to walk, was culminating in this event. I so wanted to do well.

At sign in, I received my complementary balls, golfing.au polo shirt, which I still wear with immense pride to this day, and tee times. I would play Royal Hobart on Monday and Tuesday, and Tasmania on Thursday and Friday. General opinion was that this was the best order, Hobart being acknowledged as being easier than Tasmania.

I had been given a handicap of eighteen, so bogey golf was all that was needed, break ninety and judging off last year's scoring then playing to my handicap would put me in with a major shout. Imagine then my disappointment on Friday when I failed to break ninety in any of my four rounds, but that only tells half the story, at easy Hobart – I didn't break a hundred – what a disaster.

Royal Hobart instantly reminded me of Royal Cape. The club-house, the entrance and facade, pro shop all had an old colonial feel. The course looked very brown and clearly like most of Tasmania was suffering from the drought. Indeed there were several hill fires threatening the suburbs of Hobart whist we were there. The island had been on fire alert all summer.

The course clearly had two main defences, the fairways were extremely narrow and tree-lined so anything not straight would be swallowed up by forestation; all through greens were very slick and heavily bunkered. My problems started immediately, straight drive, approach to left bunker, two in bunker, out across green into the other. Nil points for the Brit. It would begin to

Third at Tasmania.

sound like Terry Wogan on Eurovision Song night. I simply drove terribly, should really have put the driver away with hindsight, but my scoring options were effectively ruined off the tee. I did not par a hole and quite frankly, my Stableford total of just eighteen points was what I deserved. I was last – what a shambles, what a disgrace. I didn't know whether to get pissed that night or to stay sober. The Tasmanian wine won that argument. I could only get better, and did, scoring twenty-five points. I played a bit cuter but my driving was again horrendous. My playing partners were beginning to feel sorry for me. Ian Botham, Andy Flintoff, Ellery Hanley now Ian Halliwell, another Pom, getting his arse kicked Down Under.

The course was one I need to play again. If my drive would have been steady, this is a course I could go low on, of that I am sure. There were no instantly obvious super holes but that's probably because all my memories are bad ones.

The gap day saw a day trip to the fabulous and highly-rated Barnbougle Dunes on the north side of the island, which fortunately gave me an opportunity to tighten my game up. On Thursday, we headed for Tasmania Golf Club and I was still ensconced in the bottom three with the harder course to come – there had been few scores of over thirty here, such was the difficulty the course was playing. The Tasmania Golf Club is bounded by water on three sides, and is ranked at number forty-five in Australia in the latest *Golf Digest* ratings.

The course was created by curator, Ian Grimsey, under the guidance of noted course architect, Mr Al Howard. The feature hole of the course is the par five, third hole. From the championship markers, it is awe-inspiring and has been more than favourably compared to the notorious eighteenth hole at California's Pebble Beach layout. However, this is just one of eighteen challenging holes in a well-balanced combination of par threes, fours and fives for golfers of all standards to enjoy. This magnificent course was rated by the

Australian *Golf Digest* as the best in Tasmania in its survey of 'Australia's Top 100 Courses for 1999' – a title now held by Barbougle Dunes. The same magazine also rated the Tasmania Golf Club in the top ten courses constructed since 1970.

The opening nine, including the infamous third, are exceptionally difficult being played down near the coast; the par threes are, in particular, card-wreckers. On both days, I amassed just twelve points on the front nine. The back nine, more inland and culminating with a fine 200-yards par three uphill to the fine club-house, saw my best golf with a score of eighteen points both days, giving me two scores of thirty points. Not brilliant on paper, but in this event, one of the better efforts. I got my one and only birdie and four pointer in Tasmania here at the thirteenth. My performance saw me rise to ninth in my particular flight. So I had avoided the ignominy of finishing last. More to the point, I had the best score from both four balls I played in, and in particular on the last day, partnered the same guy as day one, who was delighted for me, as well as pleasantly surprised by my improvement. I really rated this course; I thought it scenically aesthetic, difficult but a pleasing test. In truth, you would need your 'A Game' to score really well. Again however, I can't wait till 2010. A bit more luck with the putter here and drive well at Hobart, Ian Halliwell, Wrest Point Master, a dream perhaps.

It's not the winning, it's the taking part they say. Not so, it's both, but here I met some fine people, enjoyed myself despite my performance and both Karen and I would love to return to this most underrated of islands. The week concluded with a fantastic Gala dinner and old acquaintances won't be forgotten. Tasmanian hospitality ensured that!

Whilst in hospital in January 2007, a visitor brought me a copy of *Today's Golfer* and in it was a wonderful article on a links, a course in northern Tasmania called Barbougle Sands – highly rated is was too, voted Best New Course in the World in 2006. It became a must-play, and I did.

Barbougle is a links golf course unlike anything ever seen in Australia. You play between, over and across towering dunes, where breathtaking views and thrilling golf provides a dramatic setting that is equal to the best links courses in the world. Steve Keipert, Australian *Golf Digest* in January 2005 said, 'Barbougle is so jaw-droopingly spectacular that it will be love at first sight for even the most travelled golfer.' The course is strong enough to test the best players but fair enough to be a joy for any player. Spectacular views and some of the greatest short holes in the world, it is an eighteen-hole championship links golf course whose layout and design equals the great courses of Britain and Ireland. Geoff Slattery of *Golf Victoria* in June 2004 said, 'I am so lucky to have played such a brilliant course.'

Located on the edge of the small Tasmanian town of Bridport, Barbougle Dunes is an hour's drive north-east of Launceston, right on the wild north coast that overlooks the Bass Strait. A course for the people, Barbougle Dunes continues the tradition of the great American public courses at Pebble Beach and Pinehurst and the Old Course at St Andrews in Scotland, having no members. Everyone is welcome to play and enjoy the first-class club-house facilities.

The following, taken from *Planet Golf,* does some justice to one of the finest courses on the planet, whilst I was still not playing well, I played to my handicap and shot eighty-nine and felt after the hell of Hobart I had gone to heaven.

Occupying a two-mile stretch of giant sand dunes along Bass Strait, the course was the vision of a

persistent young links fanatic who pestered, harassed and finally managed to convince a gruff potato farmer, and staunch non-golfer, to convert part of his 14,000-acre Barbougle farmland into a golf course.

American Tom Doak was the chosen architect and although the first business model for the development failed, Doak was so eager to build the course that he offered a long-term payment plan for his services, a gesture that managed to convince the landowner to proceed with the development himself.

Working with local partner Michael Clayton, Doak set about shaping the curving beachside sandhills into a quality links. Crucial to the design was a decision to opt for a central Club House, which meant holes could be laid out in a loop on either side. This prevented a long continuous stretch into the strong winds and allowed for the closing holes to play right along the beach. Routed mostly through dense valleys, the outward half occupies the heavier dunes, although it opens with a couple of holes on the flatter farming land. The short par four 3rd, its drive partially obscured across a diagonal ridge, is the first hole that dives into the sand.

The next is a drivable par four and the first real jaw-dropper, the hole dominated by a massive bunker embedded into a steep hillside, which must be carried in order to get near a green resting within a deep dune bowl. Remaining front nine highlights include a side-slope approach into the 9th and the evil short 7th, which swings back into the prevailing winds to a tiny crowned green that is protected a by a deep trap left

and steep banks both long and right.

Setting out in an eastern loop, the inward nine is built across broader, more expansive undulations and heads toward a tidal inlet before turning west and returning to the clubhouse alongside Barbougle beach. Both of the par four finishing holes are strong, while the excessively humped skyline green at the 10th and the reachable 12th, with its enticing target sitting on a ledge, are also noteworthy. The best of the back nine, however is the 15th, a world-class mid-length par four played along the inlet and its adjacent dune right. Those able to find a sliver of fairway on the right here are given the best angle into a narrow green that falls sharply to the left and is especially tough to hit for timid golfers straying left of the central fairway bunker.

Beyond the impressive dunes and beautiful beachside setting, the standout features at Barbougle are the bunkers and Doak's quirky greens, which are often built with smaller quadrants within the greater green shapes to allow balls to be bounced off wide slopes and fed back toward certain hole locations.

Although effective, some of the internal contours, especially on the par threes, do seem a little overdone. With the stiff sea winds that whip through the site responsible for the magnificent sand structures but also some of the most testing links conditions in the southern hemisphere, the designers sensibly left most targets open to ensure the course was manageable for all players under all conditions. The rugged bunkering is particularly striking and importantly not overused, with hollows and clever chipping zones often the preferred method of testing the inaccurate approach.

Despite its basic two-loop routing, the direction of play changes quite regularly, and once the fescue surfaces mature to present the firm conditions synonymous with golf in Britain, this will become a thorough links examination. Thanks to the vision of a young links addict, and the ability of Doak, Clayton and their teams to fashion the raw sand dunes into an exciting experience, Barnbougle Dunes is one of modern golf's great discoveries and the sort of pure, uncompromised golf project the world needs more of.

Without doubt the finest course in Tasmania, it is only minimally behind the NSW and the Royal Melbourne in terms of quality, value for money and enjoyment. If it develops a history, as it should, then this may become acknowledged as one of the greats. If this was in Scotland, it would host an Open. Being at the edge of the world may preclude the likes of Tiger ever performing here. Its their loss and that's a pity.

Sydney

Everything you've read is true – Sydney really is vibrant, bursting with creativity and sprawls lazily around a handsome sun-kissed harbour. For many of its four million-plus inhabitants, it offers a standard of living that few other cities can hope to match. It's deemed to be Australia's premier place to live: nowhere else comes close, not even Melbourne, fated to be the perpetual bridesmaid to Sydney's bride. However it's worth noting whilst Karen preferred Sydney, I much preferred the quieter more laid back, less modern, less hassled Melbourne. Sydney is without doubt more popular with overseas visitors, being regularly voted one of the world's favourite holiday destinations. In 2005, the *Los Angeles Times* proclaimed it the best place on earth to eat out, causing locals to smile contentedly at what they've known for years, only later to snarl in frustration as their favourite restaurants filled up with out-of-towners.

However, as 2005 drew to a close, the kind of publicity Sydney was getting in the local and world

media was something it could well have done without. Lurid stories of race-related violence, the threat of terrorist attacks, collapsing infrastructure and the strain put on the environment by population growth and increased development: the bad news combined to leave Sydneysiders wondering if their lucky city was so lucky after all. Sydney has probably been a victim of its own success.

I have to say whatever the merits of Melbourne, there are no more wonderful views anywhere in the world than the harbour bridge and opera house and once again we had dropped lucky. It was the first view we saw every morning from our hotel room at the fabulous and well-recommended Shangri-La Hotel which is ideally located between the Opera House and the Harbour Bridge. This is another five-star spot with undeniably breathtaking views – from every room. A $37 million refurbishment was completed in 2005. New features include the Horizon Club executive lounge on the thirtieth floor, with its eighteen metres-/sixty feet-high glass atrium, and the swanky Blu Horizon cocktail bar and Altitude restaurant on the thirty-sixth floor, both of which offer unbeatable picture-postcard views of the Harbour Bridge, the

harbour itself stretching north and the Opera House. The generously-sized rooms have a work desk and high speed internet access, plus marble bathrooms with separate bath and shower. There's also a gym and indoor swimming pool.

We were only five minutes walk from The Rocks, a long-established area near the harbour with bars, restaurants, museums, art galleries and open air markets. You can spend a pleasant afternoon and evening here and won't be disappointed. Prices are generally cheaper than those found either down at the Quay or the impressive Darling Harbour, a five

minute taxi ride by water or road in the next inlet.

The weather continued to be fine and Karen and I were thinking of heading to the beach, Bondi Beach, arguably one of the most famous and iconic in the world, when we were advised by the *concièrge* to visit Manly Beach, which in his opinion was better and allowed us to get the ferry to see the harbour fully. I spent the next hour persuading matron that she wouldn't feel sea-sick as we were only going down the river for thirty minutes, which isn't quite true, but the journey does give some stunning views of Sydney, particularly the Bridge and Opera House and it only gets rough for the last five minutes when out in open water approaching the beach.

Jumping aboard a Sydney ferry is a must, and a trip to Manly is the perfect excuse to take one of the trusty old yellow and green giants from Circular Quay to Manly Wharf in Manly Cove, where there's a small harbour beach (about 250 metres long) and a netted swimming area. To reach the open sea, you head across the busy pedestrianised street, the Corso, to the 1.5 kilometre crescent of sand known as Manly Surf Beach, but actually comprising Queenscliff in the north, followed by North Steyne, South Steyne and Manly Beaches. A mecca for mums, surfies and international tourists, Manly has all the facilities of a big resort. And plenty of history – in 1903, it was one of the first beaches to permit daylight swimming, but the crowds didn't understand the danger of the surf – there are rips along the entire length of the beach – and so fishermen, Eddie and Joe Sly, set up Manly's first life-saving patrol. We had a wonderful day here. Plenty of cheap restaurants with fine inexpensive large fish dishes. The beach was immaculate and

clean, full of local beauties to bring a smile to any hot-blooded male or female; there are plenty of hunks on display. Not a place for a UK beer-belly, although as opposed to Melbourne there was a more significant increase in the number of, I will be polite, bonnier-sized people around. I found it fascinating hearing the lifeguards shout 'Shark Alert' over the beach tannoy and no-one left the sea. Discussing this with a local, he pointed out that the shark was probably the least dangerous of all the creatures that could maim in the sea. After he finished rhyming them off, I went back to sunbathing never to return to the ocean on this trip.

That night, we went around the cove to Darling Harbour and one of these new developments in an old run-down area of the city similar to those we had seen in Melbourne and Cape Town. Very sleek and chic it was too. Casino, numerous bars and restaurants and a fine shopping mall and a very easy and flat walk around the harbour as well. I had been advised in the UK to try the award-winning Zaaffran. It's an Indian restaurant, but not as we know it. And while you might not want to enter Darling Harbour expressly to visit it, should you find yourself here already, it is definitely a superior dining option. Free-range chickens issuing from the tandoori? Semolina-crusted barramundi with turmeric, lime, ginger and chilli. The menu certainly wouldn't go down well in Wigan or Bradford for that matter but eating out on a warm balmy night overlooking the harbour, it hit all the right spots. Quite an extensive wine list too.

What we were noticing in Australia was that compared with South Africa and the USA, other great wine-making areas, wines were disproportionately more expensive here. Whilst beer was cheap, wines (including their own) were as dear as at home. The quality and choice were a wine connoisseur's dream.

The next day, we started to explore Sydney. Several months previously, my son had visited on a round-the-world trip. At twenty-three, he decided he and his girlfriend needed a career break. Despite my comments regarding cost, student loans, what career? they still went and climbed the Harbour Bridge in Sydney; something he said that was out of this world. I would need to be out of my skull to get up there, simply looking up made me sick. The 'Coathanger' is one hell of an impressive bridge. I think bridges are fine structures – the Humber Bridge, the Severn Bridges and the Golden Gate always make my tummy tingle – a fascination that I think developed as a child when we visited Cornwall on holiday, the adventure starting as we crossed the Tamar Bridge. We walked around Circular Quay to the Opera House. Again, one can't fail but to be amazed at this structure, rated now of course as one of the New Wonders of the World.

We ate at the quay and had to protect our sandwiches from the seagulls looking for an easy lunch. This is truly a great place to have lunch, a glass of wine and street entertainers – singers, acrobats, fire-eaters

– very similar to Covent Garden, but on a much larger scale.

That evening, we walked down to the passenger terminal where the city's outstanding restaurants are based. You can choose from fish, steak, Thai, Chinese and contemporary Australian. You are sorely tempted to call in at the first you see, as Matron and I usually do, but it only takes about half an hour to walk completely around the quay and then you can choose. Some of the restaurants put a premium on tables with views of the Bridge and Opera House.

On Saturdays, there is an open-air market at the Rocks, which is well worth visiting as there are many bargains to be found. Alternative medicine stalls mingle with customised jewellery stalls, artists with tattooists. I'm not a great shopper but this was an ethnic experience to savour.

Sydney is bustling, lively but at times intimidating. In the evening, we rarely felt comfortable just calling into a local pub, since they appeared more rufty tufty than those in Melbourne and Hobart. But as a bigger city, the entertainment was exceptional – concerts and acts on every corner. *Billy Elliot* was in town. Getting round was not as easy as Melbourne and to fully enjoy the city, you would need to really like boating, not Karen's forte, but despite this, she fell in love with the place.

New South Wales Golf Club

My visit to the New South Wales Golf Club was to be my final round in Australia and was to turn out to be the pick of my golfing tour. Whilst in Tasmania, I had been advised at the Gala Dinner by a Victorian member of the Royal Melbourne that reluctantly, he thought the NSW was probably the best course in the Southern Hemisphere and I would have a great time. He is possibly correct.

The course is situated on the rugged cliffs of Sydney's La Perouse headland and overlooks Botany Bay where Captain James Cook first sailed into Australia aboard the *Endeavour* in 1770. For golfers however, it was the visit of another intrepid British pioneer that gives this site its special historical interest, for the NSW like the Royal Melbourne is an Alistair Mackenzie course designed in 1926.

McKenzie famously wrote, 'At Sydney, I made an entirely new course for the NSW golf club at a place called La Perouse. This is a sand duned peninsula which overlooks Botany Bay and presents, I think, more spectacular views than any other place I know, with the possible exception of the new Cypress Point golf course I am doing on the Del Monte Peninsula in California.'

What a comparison. Would it stand up?

Hole Eleven.

Once again, the course was a full thirty minutes away by the now compulsory yellow cab, driven once again by a gentleman of oriental persuasion. The internal transportation of this country would simply implode without these guys.

'Where you come from,' I was greeted with as usual – I tell him but he's not interested. Does he not realise that Wigan is the sporting epicentre of the UK? No, he doesn't and does he care, not a jot.

'Where I come from?'

'Tokyo' I say.

'Further,' he replies.

'Hong Kong?'

'Further' and so on till using all my east Asian geographical knowledge, I say, 'Seoul?'

'Correct,' he says, 'I moved here in 1988.'

Trying to impress again with my sporting knowledge, I ask did he see the Olympics that year.

'Oh yes, all I hear was, go Australia go, so I went.'

'So you are Korean,' I reply.

'No, Australian,' he stated indignantly, and with that I had clearly insulted him and an uneasy air of solitude fermented the remainder of the journey. I thought how much the differing cultures here had immediately bought into the Australian Concept. If you asked a Pole or Slovak now working in the UK the same question, you would not be told they were now Brits. Equally, it was sad to see that although the white, principally European originating cultures had been readily accepted and allowed to integrate so many oriental cultures, they had treated quite abysmally the homogeneous aboriginal natives. This book is not a suitable vehicle to discuss this tragedy and treatment of an entire civilisation, save to say that in four weeks down under, Karen and I never clapped eyes on one aborigine. And the day after we left Sydney on Australia Day, the new Premier had planes sky-writing apologies to a whole culture.

We arrived at the club driving up through the Botany Bay National Park and drove to the peak of the rise where once again, I was greeted by a smart pleasant-looking modern club-house. Some of the newer UK club-houses, quite

New South Wales Clubhouse.

frankly, look like toilet blocks thrown up next to a car park. This, like Hobart and Tasmania before it, looked like a country club and was a design totally appropriate to the surroundings.

Entering the clubhouse, the main bar area overlooks the first tee and ninth and eighteenth greens and offers a spectacu-lar view of the whole course down to the sea. Wonderfully rugged and exposed, the entire course clearly offered tremen-dous views and was much more beautiful than Royal Melbourne to my eye. The pro shop was cleverly placed under the bar area at ground level with the first tee. Pro shops are much of a sameness anywhere in the world but the Aussies don't half make you feel welcome.

My round again arranged from the UK courtesy of one fax. About £100 to play, plus a buggy. I asked for a caddy and the assistant then asked would I like to take part in the ANZ Bank Charity Day for just another £30, something to do with Cancer Relief, so naturally I accepted. I was paired with an old gentleman called Joe, who originated from Bristol and had lived out there since the war, having been a

The approach to Hole Five.

POW in Burma. He must have been nearly ninety; surely I could beat him and put my disappointments of Tasmania behind me. Whilst everyone else is in a four ball and we were a two ball, we were first to tee off. Now I hate to tee off first at any time unless I have a mulligan, to be watched by over forty golfers, sat in the bar and around the tee made me feel even more nervous.

The first hole is a par four of just 321 yards; however the tee shot requires a carry of 150 yards over a wooded area and there are trees all the way left and right where the fairway ends, so straight it has to be. At about 220, the fairway rises to a small hill at the top where the green is placed. To stop the big hitters going straight for it, there are five or six cavernous bunkers stopping any approach and from the tee you can clearly see that any approach past will run through and down the other side. Joe went and was straight as he was all afternoon but his age obviously had taken its toll and he was short, he had only just cleared the wood.

'Open them shoulders up, big boy,' he shouts, 'let's show the convicts what the Brits can do.' No pressure then, any sympathy or support I may have received had now dissipated. Going back to basics, a slow back swing, quick through and hope and pray – sounds and feels solid.

'Shot, Ian' so with some confidence, I look up to see the ball clearing the woods but starting to fade slightly at about 200 at the bottom of the brew.

Once again, realising the good Doctor Alistair never intended his courses to be traversed in a buggy, we attempt to navigate through the woods to the fairway. Joe finds and hits his ball about 120 up the hill, cleverly short of the bunkers, he tells me how good he used to be, I tell him how good I could have been without my stroke. My ball is just off the fairway about 120 from the green all uphill and I have to clear the bunkers. Joe says take enough club and aim left, if you're long, it might stay up. I take a five iron and catch it sweet, it has clearly got the yardage and furthermore, a late fade that brings it right back to the centre of the green at the flag. Joe is impressed, he thinks I played it. His approach goes well left and we drive up the hill. There's something exciting for any golfer approaching a blind green. The anticipation of where your ball is and whether or not it is your ball or maybe your partner's is always exhilarating. In this instance, the one just in the fringe at the back of the green, just ten feet from the flag is clearly mine. I am delighted. Joe fluffs his chips and picks up. I line my putt up and survey the view straight back to the club-house. I have a shot so aim for the bin lid. I have not putted brilliantly on this trip but have found the speed quickly on all the greens. I tap forward. In truth, I over-hit to get the ball through the fringe but this slows it up and it rolls to within four inches, tap in par four and two points. The Poms are back in town!

The second hole is one of the bland par threes that occasionally seem to appear on the most special of courses. It's as if the course was designed from nine through to three – that's where we want the first hole, let's simply link one to three with a par three. At 200 yards, it is very flat to a very large green with a huge bunker on the right. Heavy gorse at the rear means the task is simple to hit the green. Joe points out that, as at the Royal, the par threes all run to the four compass points; he tells me he has used everything from an eight-iron to a driver at this hole. I use my rescue and aim for the bunker, anticipating a fade. I pitch just short right and the ball runs to the back of the green about a cricket length from the hole. Joe gets up and down for a four and again I judge the pace superbly, lagging the ball three-foot to the right. I survive a wobble on the hole and enjoy another par and three points.

The third is a par four at 416 yards, sharp ninety-degree left dog-leg. It is a blind drive over a thicket of gorse and brush, you cannot see the fairway. The book says the fairway starts at 190 yards and it's uphill. I hit a solid drive that flies straight down the middle. I must be A1. Joe bails out right, unable to clear the trees he plays to a clearance but he's probably now further away than before. He hits two more before he is back on the fairway. I am disappointed my ball has only just crept onto the short stuff. I check the yardage book. The drive felt longer than 190. Joe thinks I may have caught the trees on the corner of the dog-leg, I concur, no blooming luck, perhaps I'm a wimp. The second shot is about 130 yards all uphill to a raised narrow green, well-protected front and back by bunkers. I decide to chase a rescue and hit the ball sweet, its pin high but as can happen on links when hitting a runner can take bad bounces. This did and trickled into the front left bunker. The flag is only three paces from the back bunker so I can't be too aggressive and guess what, I leave it in. Second time, I don't worry, it's amazing how many times the second shot comes out well and will stop about eight feet below the pin. If that had been my first, I believe I would have holed the putt for a par, but no such luck, two putts later and a six for just one point.

The fourth hole commences a run to the turn of exceptional quality holes. The fourth is 420 yards, driving over a valley and onto a climb with the green again perched on top of the rise. This is the first hole where I have felt able to cut loose. So with a full swing of my driver and I do manage to unleash the beast, it flies off the middle and careers up the hill running off the fairway into the light rough at about 270 leaving 150 all uphill to go. It was perhaps my best drive on tour and I followed it with a five iron to the front of the green, nice two putts and my third par and three more Stableford points. The fifth has to be one of the great holes anywhere in the world. A straight par five of 510 yards, you drive blind across a ravine and over an enormous rise. From the summit of the fairway, the hole plunges almost 100 feet down towards a tiny green and the Pacific Ocean. This view of falling fairway and crashing waves is awesome. My drive was again straight and true and cleared the ravine and stopped just short of the down slope at about 280 yards. Another ten yards on the carry would have comfortably added 100 on the drive. The pros must love this hole, if they hit it straight. About 240 left but all downhill, I went to my trusty five-wood and hit a boomer, I thought I'd nailed it, but Joe chirps up, 'Wind will kill that near the ocean,' and it did, leaving me twenty yards short. A nice chip and two easy putts, another five and three points and ready to play the signature hole.

The sixth is an all or nothing hole played over the ocean. It's the distinguished forerunner of the sixteenth at Cypress Point. This is truly a great par three, played from a rocky outcrop behind the fifth green to a small sloping target back on the mainland. You walk across a little bridge to reach the tee; since my illness my balance is not great and I was a bit queasy stood on the tee. It is 195 to the green, so into the wind I take my driver and decide to hit a fade. I aim right of the green away from the water and hope to be pin high away from the bunkers. I am

Tee, Hole Four.

The approach to Hole Five.

playing this as a four and that's what I get after a nice lob wedge, I leave myself a twelve-footer which lips out. Joe, who read it perfectly for me, is more disappointed than I am, but two more points in the bag.

Completing an absolutely stunning stretch along the coast is the uphill par four seventh at 410 yards. We had now caught up with three Japanese visitors in front, two ladies and a man who waved us through. The drive uphill and blind involved a carry of 160, over a forest where clearly Mr Nippon had hit his ball. Joe did not bother, clearly he was enjoying a day in the sun, not for him to lose any more balls. I placed my Titleist Pro VI at £4 per ball on the tee with some trepidation and thought there must be a bad drive soon. Not this time, I creamed it and it sailed over our Japanese friends to somewhere in the fairway.

'Awesome,' intimated Joe, driving past the man, Mr Nippon muttered 'beast'. We entered the clearing and onto the fairway, where the two Japanese ladies stood applauding next to what I thought was my ball. Bit too friendly but never mind. Joe spoke in Japanese and drove off, 'you're up here big boy' and at about 250, the fairway sloped down right to left and at the bottom at least 300 of the tee was my ball. Now that was my best drive in Australia. I then hit an eight-iron to the heart of the green, leaving an uphill birdie putt. I then took the opportunity to discuss with Joe his POW days and whether he had forgiven the Japanese for his undoubted trials and tribulations.

'Would not want them as my friends, but sure don't want them as my enemy. I am too old to bear grudges.' I was truly humbled by his compassion. Perhaps because I was so relaxed when I got to the green, I rammed the putt home – my first birdie and four points. Back in the fairway, my new admirers stood applauding at my putt. Joe, looking at my bag with my name on it laughed, 'They will be back in Tokyo saying they let Ian Halliwell play through and they saw you get a birdie. They will be googling to see who the hell you are!'

The eighth is the longest hole on the course at 550 yards. There is a rise at about 320 yards which the pros and I will try and get over – not to be, I took my five wood to clear the rise and tugged it left, my first really wayward shot of the round. I was still left about 90 from the green coming into a narrow area between three bunkers. In the bunker too to get out, I holed a twenty footer for six and two points. The ninth is a short par four of 370 yards again driving blind over woods to a right to left sloping fairway. A solid hit left me about 140 from the pin. A six-iron approach to the back right bunker, but practice makes perfect, straight out safe and sound, two putts for a five and two points.

Joe was getting excited. 'Think you have a chance … gross forty, twenty-two points …'

The tenth a 400-yards par four sees a tee shot into a valley then a second to a heavily bunkered narrow green, again perched on top of a rise. The fairway was again another 170 yards carry and at this stage, I asked Joe why he played here when he could not reach so many fairways.

'Didn't realise we were off back tees, if I were on 'me todd' I'd play off ladies,' he quipped and belly-laughed. I noticed he still had a south west dialect after all these years. Again, I drove solid, neat approach but again found sand, Joe thought I was pulling slightly because I was not used to playing so many shots off a significant slope. Once again like the ninth, I escaped safely without threatening the hole and two putted for safe five and two points.

The eleventh was at the top of the estate and is a 165-yards par three from the peak of the top of every sand dune. Whilst the hole was relatively nonedescript, and the bunkers, four of them were not really in play, the view was quite stunning. I hit a five-iron pin high about twenty feet away and thought I had nailed a second birdie but left it an inch short. Still as Joe remarked, an easy par, three more points. The twelfth was a par five of 527 yards and I had started to realise a fundamental difference between here and the Royal was the way I was playing the fives. At Melbourne, I parred them all, here although the distances were the same, I was having greater difficulty.

Again, the fairway rose sharply at about 250 yards, so this would pose no problem for Greg and chums. I had however, used all my monster drives and was slightly disappointed to be on the rise at about 220 yards. Playing blind I hit my three wood about 200 but right into a sandy area about ninety from the green. I hit a loose wedge into the only bunker guarding the green on the right, no problems getting out the bunkers by far the most forgiving I had played, but practice makes perfect. Two putts, a bogey six net five and two more points.

The coastal loop on the back nine from thirteen to sixteen has often been described as world class, culminating within a sand wedge of where Cook first stepped ashore. These four holes are all extremely difficult par fours and are played along and away from the cliffs. This gives some stunning terrain and views of the ocean and some quite awesome and exhilarating golf. Joe believes this is the best stretch of golf in Australia and said my card would be made or wrecked in the next half hour.

The thirteenth at 410 yards, is slight downhill initially, then a climb up a dog-leg left, extremely narrow fairway falling right to left to the sea. I hit my natural fade but despite this the ball ran out of fairway about 220 yards leaving an uphill fairway wood. To protect my score, I use my five knowing I am unlikely to reach, hoping for a pitch and putt and at worse, a five for two points which I get after missing a twenty footer. The green was wonderfully exposed on the coast making my pitch a lottery. The fourth is probably the best of this group at 350 extremely short but with a tee shot that is blind across a wild fairway ridge into a hidden valley, followed by probably one of the great pitch shots onto an exposed skyline bunkerless green. My drive unbelievably finishes on an acute downslope. How the ball stopped there I do not know. It's defying gravity. It makes the pitch infinitely more difficult and I skull it a bit and it rolls over the green. Pitch back to six feet but I miss the putt. Bogey five, two points but I feel I missed an opportunity, especially as the fifteenth is stroke index one at 407 yards not long but the drive is the key. The hole demands a straight tee shot through a narrow shute of dunes and tea trees to reach a saddle at the fairways crest.

Messing up will mean reloading, while a good drive can set up an uninterrupted view of a beautiful green site, protected by three bunkers. My drive finishes under the saddle, so I am playing blind from about 170 to the pin. My five wood leaves me right of the green pin high. I lob wedge to ten inches and tap in for an easy par.

Joe is elated, and I am quite chuffed. 'El Bandito,' he roars, questioning my handicap. 'Just three to go, mate, and you will be in with a shout.'

I must admit I was starting to get a bit

Hole Six.

giddy. I would take three bogeys now. The sixteenth is a 440 yards dog-leg left and it's where my round nearly came to a complete calamity. I hit a good drive away from the corner to the far apex of the turn at about 250 just running off the fairway. I was about to play my second to what I perceived to be the green about 180 away on top of a ridge, every green so far has been on top of a rise or so it seemed. Half way through my back swing, I hear a loud shout from Joe; I am only aiming for the seventeenth green. The sixteenth is in a valley approaching Captain Cook's Waterhole. On 29 April 1770, Captain Cook dropped anchor just inside the headlands on the southern shore of Botany Bay, seeking to replenish his water supply. He was unable to locate fresh water on the south side so he despatched a boat to the northern shores where suitable water was located in Captain Cook's waterhole. This soak is just 200 yards from the seventeenth tee and is clearly visible. I was within a whisker of ruining my score, but then proceeded to hit a five wood onto the green two putts and a par four and three Stableford points. I had gone through the loop in just two over and with ten points secured.

The seventeenth is a short par three, so I took the opportunity to walk to the waterhole, not much to see but an unbelievable feeling of historic importance akin to the feeling I got at the Coliseum, the Parthenon and Chichin Itza. Some people won't get that but my tummy tingles when I stand on historic spots of significant world importance.

The seventeenth at 170 is atop a ridge and is very average apart from the views. The difficulty is that it is so exposed; I felt the wind here for the first time since the sixth really. I am in between clubs and with wind against hit a four iron quite well but it runs through the back and into some heavy rough. Average pitch and two putts result in an extraordinary bogey and two points, made worse by Joe's birdie and we go to the eighteenth with him claiming the honour for the first time since the first.

The eighteenth is a par five at 550 yards. It would be relatively easy for the pros. I noticed later that this hole was due to be lengthened, water added and the green moved to a position under the club-house. Joe explained that the committee had been advised that they needed a natural amphitheatre for the eighteenth and a more difficult final hole if they wished to get some of the tour events back from Melbourne. I played routinely boringly. Drive to 240, five wood to about 100 from green. Nine-iron right of green, chip and two putts another six. The back nine completed in forty-two and twenty-one points. I shot eighty-two for forty-three points, surely in with a chance.

The next hour seemed much longer, for early on a youngster came in with forty-six points, but after that my forty-three was never threatened. I always think finishing second in a Stableford event is ideal. No-one ever thinks you're a bandit, because that's reserved for the victor and indeed most players feel sorry for you because they assume you have been robbed of your rightful victory. I do finish second and receive a nice memento and medal and as Joe made clear to all, struck one for the much-maligned Brits!

And so on to Hong Kong and the last part of my challenge to play on every continent, again after a tremendous round here, the golfing demons had something totally different lined up for me in Asia.

Since my return, I have been asked to assess how good the NSW course was when compared to the Royal. I did enjoy the NSW more from a strict golfing perspective, but then I won something. The course had some stunning views which surpassed any course I had played on. I am sure that the terrain and layout provides an unrivalled site for a course and the wind, not much of an issue when I played, ever-changing in strength and direction, would produce a stern test for golfers of all categories as is Dr Mackenzie's want. However, it lacks the history and probably the future of the Royal, something which to me has infinite worth and probably made the day in Melbourne as a whole, more pleasurable.

It would be interesting to see what the Good Doctor would think if he could re-examine the courses now, which would he prefer? I believe that if you could put the perfection of the Royal's greens at Melbourne onto the NSW course you would have the ideal golf course. I cannot choose between them. It was the highlight of my golfing life to play both, and I was truly blessed.

Golf is an amazing challenge. I had played the Royal and NSW really well, and drove brilliantly. Yet at Wrest Point, which after all was the principal reason I came to Australasia, at two less-rated and certainly easier courses, I had driven in particular like a Tyro and had not broken ninety in any of the four rounds. But sat at home now in the cold UK, to coin Arnie, I will be back, and Tasmania, I intend to return and do my self justice in 2010. Think I'll look at New Zealand on the way back. A social golfer always looks for opportunities.

11. Hong Kong

We flew out of Sydney and on to Hong Kong – courtesy once again of magnificent Cathay Pacific first-class. Sydney airport was like so many of the overseas airports we have recently visited, so much easier to get through and round than our UK ones. Manchester and Heathrow are doing something wrong!

The flight was turbulence-free, punctuated by the odd glass of wine or three and I was not mistaken for an '80s icon this time, although we were asked whether we were related to Geri at all. The hostess wondered if she was my sister. She thought we looked alike. I was indignant, but Karen said it could be worse, she could have thought I was her dad! At least on this flight I did feel I justified such pampering since I had left Sydney as a winner – well, OK, a runner-upper then.

I was looking forward to Hong Kong. I am not sure what I expected but our arrival that morning was to some of the worst weather that eastern Asia had suffered for many years. It was damp, drizzly and smoggy. You could taste the air as it entered your lungs. If this is what it was going to be like in Beijing later that year for the Olympics, then no wonder there were worries for the long- distance runners. I was wheezing and very chesty simply walking from the terminal to our transport to the hotel. Our driver explained that mainland China was in the midst of a major snow storm and that we were on the tail end. China was at a standstill. Chinese New Year could be a disaster. At this stage, I realised my planning had not been too brilliant for this trip. We left Sydney the day prior to Australia Day and Hong Kong the day before Chinese New Year. Not really clever that, however perhaps that's why first-class was so cheap. Who's a clever boy then! The trip from the airport to Kowloon should have been memorable, but instead it portrayed the city as a concrete monstrosity, grey with small miserable-looking people scurrying around

like ants. Our initial perceptions were not favourable and did not do the vibrant economic colony justice at all. Our mood changed when we arrived at our hotel, the amazing Harbour Plaza Hotel on the quay front at Wantau Quay. The view over to Hong Kong Island was a fine one even through the mist, and the hotel was simply fantastic – five top-notch restaurants, Chinese, Thai, French, buffet and English pub food. There is a roof top pool with glass sides that make it appear as if you are

The lobby, Harbour Plaza.

swimming off the roof top. An English bar with Boddingtons Beer, what a stereotypical anglophile I sound like. Our room overlooked the river. I find it very therapeutic watching ships go by, like watching tropical fish in a tank, I suppose.

The pool on the roof of the Harbour Plaza.

The Kowloon peninsula is just a few square kilometres in size, but it is one of the most crowded (500,000 per square kilometre, or 200,000 per square mile, according to our count) and developed areas in the world. At the southern end is Tsim Sha Tsui (pronounced chim-sa-choi), once a sharp, sandy point and now a hyper-active shopping district. Further north are the more traditional districts of Yau Ma Tei and Mong Kok, where street markets and old buildings have escaped demolition. Kowloon is, in many ways, very different from the glittering island across the harbour, more down-to-earth and more Chinese. Yet, somewhat paradoxically, Tsim Sha Tsui – its southern tip – is the location of the majority of Hong Kong's tourist hotels. Nathan Road is host to the quintessential Hong Kong image of gaudy neon signs and hundreds of small electronics shops. Save for the waterfront views, it is not an especially attractive place. But few can deny the electricity that charges life here, especially at night.

Hong Kong pulsates with the visual energy of a fireworks display. It resonates to the din of a dim sum restaurant's peak hour. Pulsating, at times chaotic, intriguing, puzzling, and endlessly exciting and in parts possessed of an astounding alternative beauty, Hong Kong is a place that precipitates the strongest emotions. More than one visitor has noted that this must be one of the earth's acupuncture points. Despite this vibrancy in the cold and wet of an Asian storm, the place lacks beauty. It is noticeable how in every corner in any gap there is a tree or a bush, anything to give colour and life to an otherwise man-made lifeless, soulless existence. With 7,422 high-rise buildings (over thirteen storeys), Hong Kong has more skyscrapers than any city in the world, easily beating second place New York's 5,445. The city does come to life in the evening when it appears every citizen hits the streets.

Buddhist Temple.

A 2005 global survey revealed that Hong Kong has more night owls than anywhere else in the world except Portugal (no wonder Slasher and Mike like the Algarve!). Sixty-six percent of the city's population is still awake after midnight and thirty-one per cent stay up beyong 1 a.m. Hong Kong is fuelled and inspired by constant immigration, from mainland China, from elsewhere in Asia and the four corners of the world, with seven million souls simultaneously focused on top dollar and bottom line in an area rather smaller than the English county of Berkshire and less than half the size of the American state of Rhode Island. Cosmopolitan yet integrally Chinese, Hong Kong's inhabitants are defined by what's written on their business cards. Off duty, they may go shopping, play tennis and basketball on courts perched on top of skyscrapers, or pinball their way between the bars and clubs crammed hugger mugger in the numerous nightlife zones; a local tourist guide explained to Karen and I why everyone went out at night. Quite simply, the average family lived in an apartment smaller in size that an English family's front room. There was simply no privacy and that's why most residents work such long hours and then party so long at night. Wages were very low, and holiday entitlement was less than ten days in the year, four of which usually taken around Chinese New Year. The vast majority live like that but mix that with the decadence of the extremely wealthy who waltz around town similar to the posers found in Puerto Banus. The rich in their chariots look the same whether European or Asian. That 'look at me, I am rich and I know it and so do you' kind of attitude is truly global.

We decided to go on a day trip to the New Territories, the bit of land above Kowloon connected to mainland China. This is a peculiar area – densely populated with high-rises of immigrant workers fuelling the ever-growing Hong Kong economy, luscious green forest plantations and little towns and villages with communities dating back to the nineteenth century. We visited a Buddhist temple, which was naturally serenity itself, but quite stunning and beautiful and it is always somewhat fascinating to hear first-hand about how other people and, in particular religions operate.

I did not realise for example that mainland China spoke a different language and indeed worshipped a different sect of Buddhism. We visited small villages inhabited by old ladies who had been deserted by their husbands in the Second World War and had never returned. Women have little or no rights In the New Territories. If a man dies without a male heir, his assets do not go to his wife or daughters but back-track to the nearest male surviving relative. We visited the famous Wishing Trees where for years locals have pinned their wishes to the tree for good luck. Karen and I did as well, and all mine came true and so did hers. So perhaps there is something in this folklore tale.

This is a complex, ever-changing country and society; clearly there is an issue with Singapore's apparent resurgence as the area's principal economic strength. The airport does not carry as many passengers now as Singapore, the docks carry less tonnage; it all seems to matter a lot here, even to the average worker. It seems a matter of honour and principle not to be outshone.

Our best times were in the evening, walking in the city, calling in at the local restaurants and eating with the local community. When in Rome and all that. We had some super meals that were unbelievably cheap.

With some of the old ladies of the New Territory.

We did have trouble finding European restaurants away from the hotel and you won't find alcohol so readily available. Bars are not easily identifiable and away from the hotel strip are quite frankly very intimidating. We are both very sure that, had the weather been better, our opinion of the city would have been very different. We had a good time, but did not really feel we had found or understood Hong Kong at all. We had simply become one of those ants scurrying around.

Trying to play golf here was to provide a major challenge. The islands are home to several prominent private clubs, the leading one being the Hong Kong Club at Fanling where the PGA play tournaments and Miguel Jiminez always seems to win the Hong Kong Open. There are newer private clubs at Discovery Bay and Clearwater, all highly rated but you can't seem to get on them. I tried every connection I had and could not get on.

There is one municipal in the islands called the Jockey Club, I assume because it was initially run by the racetrack. Imagine living in a city like Liverpool and the only golf course being on the Isle of Man. Well that's the situation here except the course is a bit nearer. Nicola had arranged for me to play in a competition on the North Course, teeing off at noon. That's when the fun started. Having breakfast at eight, I asked the concièrge to find me a taxi, and he pointed out that it was a taxi, ferry and then bus to the course and if I needed to tee off at twelve then I had better get off now. I was all for calling it a day, it was pouring down as well, but Matron took over. We had not come all this way to fail at the final hurdle. She booked a taxi and off we went. We arrived at the docks and eventually ascertained after much difficulty in translation that a boat would be along in five minutes to take us to the island and its golf courses. Suddenly out of thin air about forty golfers materialised and started to queue for a non-existent boat, and we were now in danger of not getting on. The Chinese are a respectful race and seeing my plight, we were suddenly passed to the front of the boat. Karen, not being the best sailor, simply sat on the front never looking at the very choppy sea once. We arrived at the quay on the golf course after a very rough thirty minute crossing. A mini bus transferred us up to a very impressive club-house at the peak of the island from which you could see the north and south course and the east currently a month away from opening. In gorgeous weather, the

Jockey Club.

Jockey Club, Asian PGS trophies.

place would have had no peers but today sadly, like any wet golf course, it looked uninviting. I booked in and asked for a buggy so a wet and cold Karen could come round with me only to be told the competition was on the north course and no buggies were allowed. We had come all this way and were about to be stopped from playing golf in Asia at the death. Karen said to go and she would wait, but in these conditions, I certainly was not up to walking around even with a caddy. Fortunately, Chinese efficiency took over again and the receptionist suggested I play the slightly easier south course. I could have a buggy and Karen could drive as my caddy, but she would have to wear a caddy bib and hire golf shoes. Her sandals were not allowed. She was quite happy with that as her legs were like blocks of ice, so socks and shoes did alleviate her discomfort somewhat. So I was to play in Asia, if not competitively. That would have to wait till Dubai later in the year.

The location of the Jockey Club is supreme, and when the weather did improve, the views were sensational – island coves and beaches reminded you of *The Plane* or the Bond Film, *The Man With the Golden Gun*. Like the rest of the break here, the weather did dampen the spirits. The course was fine, with a short first nine which is followed by a much more difficult, longer back nine which I played better as the rain and wind dropped. All the par threes were memorable. From the second, a downhill 100 foot drop to the sixth on a plateau green and the twelfth to a raised green with views to die for and culminating at the sixteenth, a 180 yards carry over water. As one would expect from the Chinese, the round went exactly to time of four hours ten, despite the fact I thought it seemed slower. Sadly at the end, we were both wet through, despite customising our buggy with two umbrellas. Karen dried herself under the hand set in the toilet and apparently set a trend with the locals who all followed suit. I do believe that this facility, unique in its location, unique in its availability as a municipal, ranks as one of the strangest day's golf I have ever played. On a nice day with friends, I am sure it would be up there with the best.

Back in the hotel, I got chatting to a German who had been to play at Mission Hills that day, the amazing ten course complex that held the '08 World Cup won by Scotland's Montgomerie and Warren. It was two hours away by car. Furthermore that night he was off to the casinos at Macau, now bigger than Las Vegas, one hour away by boat.

Clearly as a social golfing trip, Karen and I had not even started to make inroads.

12. South Africa

Cape Town

For our next visit to South Africa, Slasher, Mike, Skitty and I all agreed to take our partners. Having spoken to them all, the consensus was to try and include Cape Town in the itinerary and so it was that we arrived in Cape Town, South Africa in late October, their early spring. The South Africans really need to speed up their immigration desks but it did give me an opportunity to wind the Skitts' up. On a previous visit, Steve had hired the car which subsequently the hire company attempted a late spurious mileage charge on. Steve instructed his credit card company not to pay, on my advice, and had subsequently forgotten all about it. That is until he was about to have his passport stamped.

'Don't worry,' I exclaim, 'We will look after Chris if they arrest you for non-payment.' Not as unlikely as it sounds as a work colleague who had picked up a speeding ticket was arrested on a subsequent visit at passport control. Steve slid to the back of the queue in blind panic. He would still be there if I hadn't convinced him I was joking.

However, you arrive at Cape Town, by air, rail or sea, you cannot fail to be mesmerised by Table Mountain. Called the Mothers' City, Cape Town was the first white settlement in South Africa, from which colonisation spread north through southern Africa and beyond. Its position near the tip of Africa had

undeniable strategic value, as did its sheltered bay, but another irresistible draw must have been its wonderful flat-topped mountain, so mysterious when seen from the sea. A beacon to early mariners, in Xhosa legend, it was *Umlindi Welingizunu*, the 'Watcher of the South.' To this day, in spite of the hustle and bustle of modern city living, Table Mountain's majestic and ancient presence impinges on the consciousness, whichever way one turns. For visitors, it is the symbol of South Africa, more potent than wine, rugby or cricket, more famous than the Kruger National Park.

We had decided to stay at the Table Bay Hotel which is a member of the Leading Small Hotels of the World; this hotel is perfect for those who want big service, big views and big rooms. The services on offer range from a personal butler to a fully equipped state-of-the-art gymnasium. Little wonder that it attracts so many international celebrities and me. Take time out in the Camelot Spa after a day's sightseeing followed by a sumptuous meal at the Atlantic Restaurant. It is right on the recently-developed Victoria and Albert waterfront. Like most old cities, the planners in their wisdom had taken an old run-down dock area and developed it into a fine modern retail and entertainment centre in a wonderful setting with awesome views of Table Mountain.

Open your bedroom curtains to see the top of the mount shrouded in a veil of clouds, look down to the harbour to see the hustle and bustle and also the harbour seals lolling about waiting to be photographed. The hotel was once again exceptional. With the value of the rand, we were staying in five-star opulence at British Bed and Breakfast prices. The V & A has a plethora of restaurants and bars, fine shops and is handily placed for all excursions. It seems the best place to stay in Cape Town. Known locally as the Waterfront, the revitalised harbour of Cape Town, historically one of the world's busiest ports, is a model of how to breathe life back into a dying area without losing its original function or sacrificing its character. It is still a harbour with a thriving ship repair business, but it has a range of new uses, among which shopping, dining and entertainment are prominent.

The V & A Waterfront is home to hotels, restaurants and cafes, museums, an aquarium and craft work-shops. It has a buzzing street life, and there are buskers, trees to sit under, benches overlooking the water, and covered shopping areas (the shops here remain open until about 8 p.m.) selling everything from the latest Italian fashions to fresh fish. You could come here simply for an evening stroll along the quays.

Alternatively, you can test-drive the latest BMW, listen to music, meet your friends, watch movies, taste local wines, read the works of South Africa's new and upcoming authors, sail your yacht or catch a helicopter for a trip around the Cape peninsula.

Slasher and Mike went up in a helicopter and thought it exhilarating, spectacular and great value for money. Karen and Echo went whale-watching. Karen suffers immensely from sea sickness so I was surprised Echo convinced her to go whilst we were golfing. A cheap trip on what looked a placid sea taking two hours, turned out to be a nightmare. Out in the Atlantic or Indian Ocean, the sea turned particularly nasty. The journey took four hours in treacherous conditions. Echo saw the whales; Karen threw up continually and was frozen to the bone. Echo recommends it, Karen says, 'You can shove it, go to the Aquarium and watch a film instead!'

There is so much to do and see in this area; some come to the city to see the mountain, the beaches, the wine lands and the unique flora, and to experience life in the townships, which embody such a rich chunk of South Africa's cultural, historical and political identity. The food is delicious and so cheap and varied as the Cape offers such a choice of reasonably-priced restaurants, The Cape Towner's eat early be warned, and most restaurants are closed by ten, but thankfully they drink late. We also explored the colourful Bo-Kaap, the traditional Muslim quarter on the slopes of Signal Hill. One cannot fail to be impressed with the colonial architecture that developed at the time, Cape Town was probably no bigger than a very small country town in Europe. The Cape Dutch heritage is unique, and Cape Town is the best place to experience it, though you'll also see fine examples in nearby Stellenbosch. A trip to Robbens Island where Nelson Mandela was incarcerated is highly recommended, but the one trip you must do is the Cable Car to the top of Table Mountain. The views here will live with you for the rest of your life.

For any social golfer, the food and beer is always paramount in assessing a place. The biggest concentration of restaurants is in the city centre and along its edges in Kloof Street, the Waterfront, and in the Gardens and Green Point districts. These are Cape Town's older neighbourhoods, and some of their restaurants have a vulnerable vintage. There are first-class restaurants in most of the top hotels – the Mount Nelson, the Cape Grace and the Table Bay among them. Service has traditionally been poor, but it is improving, not least because waiting staff depend on their tips (expect to tip ten percent on top of the bill). City venues have been criticised for refusing to serve tap water or for charging for it (it should be freely available). Smoking is illegal in restaurants, although some have dedicated smoking sections. Definitely check with the waiter before lighting up.

A livelier place, but not one the ladies felt comfortable in, was the diverse attraction of Long Street 16, which is the most famous – some would say infamous – street in Cape Town. It links mountain and sea, and you can stand with your back towards the mountain at one end and see ships berthed at the dock at the other. Table Bay and the coast at Blouberg can be seen away in the distance. For a long time, it represented the heart and soul of this maritime city, and today it has many faces. Anything, and everything, happens here. There are delis, cafés, restaurants, all-day bars, nightclubs, churches and two mosques, vintage clothing shops, bookshops, antiques and bric-à-brac shops, markets, pharmacies, banks, pawn and porn shops, apartment blocks, hotels, backpackers' lodges and offices. The tone of the street ranges from smart to seedy to downright sleazy, and this is the very essence of Long Street. Over the years, there have been attempts to tidy it up, rid the pavement of the drunks, transvestites and the prostitutes (and the street children) but somehow change has always been resisted.

The best value restaurant we encountered was at Willoughby's, V & A Waterfront. It may be situated deep inside the V & A's main shopping centre, with no ocean views, but this venue serves the best fish in town and is always packed. Come here for a broad range of impeccably prepared dishes, from sushi to good old English-style fish and chips with a glass of champagne. You can't book, so just turn up and wait your turn. It also sells déli items and wet fish. We did not have one bad meal anywhere it has to be

admitted though. After a meal, there are plenty of bars but for a more relaxed end to the evening try Manenbergs (Tel: 021 421 5639) at the Clock Tower, for a mellow evening of good jazz and good wine.

As I have found on all my travels most big city hotels can sort and organise your days out for you. The Table Bay was no exception. They arranged transport and tee times. We had decided to play Royal Cape because of its history and my next challenge to play all the Royals! Steenburg, which had been highly recommended by the golf pro at my club Standish, and I liked their wines! And Stellenbosch again highly recommended. We could not however get on here as the Eisenhower trophy was being played that week.

To make the golf interesting, we had decided to play as pairs in a better ball match play. Slasher and Mike against me and Skitty. I give them six shots; they were to give Steve a shot a hole. It made for a very competitive week to say the least. The Royal Cape was what I expected a golf nut's paradise to be. I walked endlessly through the club-house looking at all the old memorabilia and photos. Wasted on the others but what was not wasted was the hospitality at the nineteenth with waitress service and endless cheap beers.

When we started, Mike had clearly had a few and was in the midst of a gigantic fourteen-day bender trying to drag Slasher with him. On the first tee, a straight par four, watched by twenty or so members waiting to start their daily medal, he totally lost his swing and dribbled the ball just five yards, not clearing the ladies. Not sure if anyone else has ever dropped his trousers on the first at the Cape but Mike did. The Cape, a fine well-maintained course in the valley under the mountain, offers an interesting challenge without being over difficult and ruthlessly un-enjoyable. It has the right balance. Around it has been some urbanisation with nice houses and villas – right up to the fairway edges in places. Mike, both here and in Steenburg, became an expert on realtor values and prices as he visited gardens, kitchens, lounges and

even bedrooms in a display of inaccurate driving that had to be seen to be believed. 'Don't Drink and Drive' never can have been truer. Amazingly at the Royal, we only won at the eighteenth, partly due to Kenny playing far beyond himself and Steve also having a mare. However at the last, Steve came to the party after I drove out of bounds and he played it conservatively and straight chipping to a foot and holing the putt for a two up victory. In the bus after I collected my winnings, fifty, yes fifty rand, all of £4 but it's the principle that counts.

Steenburg is situated on the wine plantation and rarely do you get an oppor-

tunity to play a round in such scenic surroundings with such a constant smell of fauna. No good if you have got hay fever, I would suggest. Not far way from Newlands, the rugby and cricket grounds, the course gives you a different angle to the mountain, still however a mesmeric and outstanding vista to contemplate if you are enjoying this glorious pastime. The course had been recommended by Stuart, my pro, and I do the same; enjoy the golf, buy some wine, eat some fine food and maybe even score well. This course does have a few special holes which will remain in the memory, and the finish is particularly grand. A short par three is followed by a long par five with water ever present. I played quite imperiously this day. Chipping in at the sixteenth for a birdie to win the match four and three. At the seventeenth, it was nearly dropped-pants time as I only just cleared the women's by a foot after scuffing my eight-iron completely, the divot going further.

We chose courses within thirty minutes of the hotel but within an hour from Cape Town are some of the finest courses on the planet – another reason to visit this most beautiful, cosmopolitan and vibrant city. We will return I think, and without doubt, Table Mountain will always remain as one of my most wonderful memories of my five continent challenge.

Steenburg, Hole Seven.

Steenburg Golf Club.

Sun City

Slasher, Mike, Steve and I revisited Sun City with our partners after our week in Cape Town. We arrived in Johannesburg after flying internally. We were met in Joburg by a limo which took us directly to Sun City. For less than a tenner each, the guy laid out a red carpet and the limo was full of beer, wine and champagne. Truly the way to travel. Just an idea of the difference between the rand and the pound was shown when we stopped half-way for a ladies – it was them, excuse me. The limo was surrounded by at least twenty locals not begging but offering to clean the car, go for water, etc., Mike gave one particularly scruffy young lad a R100 note, about £9. He was suddenly virtually attacked by the rest of the community; our driver went bananas explaining that he could be killed for that much. Sadly, it took me back to my first trip when we were instructed not to tip anyone because they would probably not work the next day, and would most likely spend it all on booze.

When we arrived at the Palace, it would be safe to say that the women were overwhelmed, the foyer with its architecture and sculptures outside and the domed roof with its painted collage of wild life is simply awesome. Any doubts we had about bringing the ladies were quickly dispelled. I think there were a few northerners on a promise that night. On our previous visit, the guys had simply visited the casino. That first

The Palace Hotel.

109

day the girls who in five minutes knew more about the place than we did, decided a walk through the gardens should be undertaken. The scale of the twenty-five hectare Lost City gardens and jungle is simply breathtaking. Creaking clusters of bamboo, the cool mist of a rainforest, the carnivorous plants of the wetland and a forest of mature baobabs. Some of these were several hundred years old – more than 1,600,000 trees, plants and shrubs, bursting forth to create a lush green cloak, highlighted by a lilac haze of jacarandas – 3,200 species make up the gardens, seventy percent have never been cultivated previously, seventy-five percent are indigenous to southern Africa. Plants from Australia, Zimbabwe, the Comores, Mozambique and Madagascar thrive in these glorious gardens. The gardens are also home to a colony of monkeys. These monkeys seemed to take a fancy to Echo and Karen, tormenting them all holiday, not helped I think by Steve constantly feeding them behind our spouses' backs.

This volcanic pleasure dome, the Lost City, was completed in December 1992 at a cost of R830 million, and took just twenty-eight months to build. During the busiest time of construction, almost 5,000 people worked on the project, 30 million bricks were used in the construction, as well as 3,300 tons of steel reinforcing rods measuring 2,900 kilometres.

Eighty-five percent of the requirements for the interior of the Palace was sourced from within southern Africa. The exquisite King's Suite features 800 custom-crafted items. Fabrics and carpets all designed and made exclusively for the Palace, will never be found anywhere else in the world. All the 338 timber bedroom doors were hand-carved. There are 50,000 square metres of carpets, 5,650 square metres of marble, 3,400 square metres of murals and 6,500 light fittings which combine to create a palace of immense proportions. Every element of tasteful design, every facet of aesthetic beauty has been incorporated within

the realms of the resort to ensure it remains one of the world's élite holiday destinations.

All this at a price which would not get you a week in Benidorm. The Palace is ostentatious, opulent but not tacky. Breakfast includes, pink champagne, duck, caviar as well as all the normal croissants or English fare. Fill up here and you don't need lunch.

Each evening, we always met in the cocktail bar and started the evening with strawberry daiquiris at less than a couple of

Facing: Sun City.

On the strawberry daiquiris.

quid each. You can really enjoy yourself here because compared with home your money seems to go so much farther. You can either be chauffeured, usually in BMWs, to the entertainment centre or enjoy a leisurely walk through the impressive Bridge of Time. Large elephant sculptures stand watch over visitors as they leave the Palace and Valley of Waves to enter the bustling entertainment centre. A simulated volcano beneath the bridge causes it to vibrate. The rugged rock facade of the centre features intricate carvings of many animals including a giant leopard which rests sphinx-like and aloof over a pillared pergola.

We discovered a water theme park that the previous year we never knew existed. The Valley of Waves is a combination of pools, meandering rivers and water features that create a water park of the most colossal proportions, as big as those at Disney in Florida, holding over twenty-three million litres of water on a man-made beach. Just more reasons why this could be the ultimate social golf resort.

Of course, we were very experienced, having all played both courses before. We continued our challenge with Skitty and I, two nil up in the series. We won at the Country Club albeit with some skulduggery on my part. On the fourteenth with us in for a bogey, Mike had a birdie putt which slipped two foot past, and normally this would have been a gimme but he simply picked up anyway. Halfway down the fifteenth, Mike claims we are one up now, just all square, I reply.

'How come,' he says, 'we didn't give you that so the last was halved.' Not my best moment I have to admit but after that, their game imploded and we took fifteen, sixteen and seventeen for a three and one

Hole Nine, Gary Player Country Club.

Holes Nine and Eighteen, The Lost City Golf Club.

win. It sadly reflects on the competitive nature of the game we were playing. The following day, our last, saw them come out with all guns blazing, I had worked them up and Mike was sober. We had our best game on the tour and it took my birdie at the last to bring the match level. We were unbeaten and their honour was intact but of course my shenanigans the previous day were still the reason they had not got level.

Once again, the crocs took their fair share of Titleists on the par three thirteenth. Whilst in Australia, I came across the following article taken from *Extreme Golf* by Duncan Lennard who rated this as one of the most exceptional holes on the planet.

Recently Borgelt [the club professional] has noticed a worrying trend with more and more golfers taking their chances in the pit. They may well have been inspired by the Sunshine Tour professional, Graeme Francis. During the 2001 Dimension Data Pro-Am, Francis shinned down into the pit, pitched onto the green, jumped out unscathed and two-putted for a bogey four. The sad denouement to this heroic tale is that Francis was later disqualified for his efforts as the tournament organisers had previously passed a local rule forbidding anyone from entering the crocodile hollow.

Borgelt and his colleagues used to retrieve at least 20 balls each on their weekly descent into the pit, but a couple of years ago the balls dried up. Confused, they wondered how the resort's golfers had improved so suddenly and dramatically. Then circumstances forced them to make an unscheduled trip back to the 13th. On reaching the pit, they discovered two caddies down there, helping themselves. The caddies later admitted that they had watched Borgelt go in, decided the crocodiles weren't as dangerous as everyone made out, and hopped down to grab some balls to sell.

Borgelt is aware that golf balls rain down on the crocodiles all day, but says that this is not a cause for concern. 'Yes, sometimes they get hit by balls, but they are far too tough for the balls to do any damage,' he confirms. 'They are practically armour-plated – though they can get a bruise if they are hit on the leg.

They do, however get startled by balls landing, and because they are creatures of instinct, the movement of a ball rolling down to the bottom of the pit can spur them into action. They take a few steps towards it, but as the ball stops moving they back off, almost as if they are not sure why they moved of in the first place.'

Although Gary Player is extremely proud of all eighteen holes on the Lost City course, he has no problem with the crocodile hole stealing the limelight. 'These amazing creatures are some of the most exquisite in all of God's creation, and they deserve special attention,' he laughs. 'The crocodiles add a unique, stimulating element to the course. There's nothing like this sort of danger and excitement during a round of golf.'

He is right, because standing on the tee is quite intimidating, though it's not a difficult shot all downhill, with no danger of long bunkers at side. I know it's just a simple seven-iron for me, one of my best clubs but four shots, four lost balls, four double bogeys! You stand there and just can't keep your eyes off the pit and the ball is attracted to it, but in anyone's language, it is truly a must-play hole on a must-play course.

13. The Social Golfer

The Social Tour

January	The Wrest Point Masters
February	The Tait Putter
August	The British Par Three Championship
September	The MRC Golf Classic
October	The Barney Barnato Festival
November	Polk County Aces Championship
	Davenport Chamber of Commerce Charity Day
December	Toys for Tots Championship

Contact details:

The Wrest Point Masters
An over 35s competition organised by Golf Australia. You must have a valid club handicap certificate as at 1 January of that year.
Contact: http://www.gogolfing.net.au
Cost (excluding flights): about £700, includes four complimentary rounds of golf plus five nights at Wrest Point Casino and all golf transfers.

The Tait Putter and Barney Barnato
The Tait is an invitation members event but from experience if you're in the area, give them a call. The Barney is open for all with a valid handicap.
Contact: Dave Wilson on 0538 410127
http://www.kimberelygolfclub.co.au
e-mail: kgc@wol.co.za
Cost: about £40 a round

The British Par Three Championship
A Pro-Am competition, valid handicap required.
Contact: http://www.britishpar3championship.co.uk
Approx cost: £1,500 including accomodation for two nights and gala meal.

The MRC Classic
A Pro-Am competition and a Celeb Team Competition
Contact: Steve Skitt 01743 282090
Email: s.skitt@mrc-recruitment.co.uk

Polk County Aces
Contact: http://www.polkworks.org
Cost: about £250 per player

Davenport Chamber
Contact: http://www.deercreekrv.com
Cost: about £40 including meal

Toys for Tots
Contact: http://www.mysticdunesgolf.com
Cost: about £50 including meal

Mr Cressman receives the Albatross Award.

The Social Golfer Ratings

The ratings are based on a combination of factors, location, quality of course, feel-good factor, the club-house facilities.

To sum up how enjoyable the experience was.

Ratings as follows, based on a par five golf hole …

Hole-in-one	Out of this world, a truly unbelievable place
Hole-in-two (Albatross)	Exceptional, very enjoyable, must visit
Hole-in-three (Eagle)	Very good, would re-visit, recommended
Hole-in-four (Birdie)	Quality club and course, a good day.
Hole-in-five (par)	Nothing exceptional but well worth a visit
Hole-in-six (bogey)	A bit of a disappointment but would give it another go
Hole-in-seven (double bogey)	Major disappointment, been there done it. Not bothered about returning.

These are purely personal views and fellow social golfers of mine would, I know, rate far differently, but each to their own and there are never any bad opinions – just those you might disagree with. That's your prerogative. I would rather have a double bogey than no round at all – been there, bought that T-shirt.

Swing well and enjoy!
Make your contribution on any course, go to
www.thesocialgolfer.net

	No	Course	Tel No	Web Site	SG Rating
Tunisia	1	Golf Citrus La Foret	+216 72 226 500	www.golfcitrus.com	4
		BP 132-8050			
		Hammamet			
	2	Citrus Lea Olivers			4
	3	Yasmine	+216 72 227 001	www.golfyasmine.com	4
		BP 61 -8050			
		Harnmamet			
	4	Flamingo	+216 73 500 283	www.golfflamingo.com	3
		BP 40 Route de Ouardanine			
	5	Djerba	+216 75 745 055	www.djerbagolf.com	3
		BP 360 Z Tourist			
		4116 Midoun			
	6	Tabarka	+216 78 670 028	www.tabarkagolf.com	4
		Rte Touristique El Morjènel			
		8110 Tabarka			
	7	El Kantaoui	+216 73 348 756	www.kantaouigolfcourse.com.tn	4
		BP 32 Station Touristique			
		4089 El Kantaoui			
		Port El Kantaoui			
	8	Palm Links	+216 73 521 910	www.golf-palmlinks.com	6
		BP 216 Monastir République			
		5060 Tunisie			
	9	Golf de Carthage	+216 71 765 700	www.tunisiagolf.com	6
		Choutrana II			
		2036 Soukra			
Costa Del Sol	10	Alhaurin	+34 952 595 800	www.alhauringolf.com	3
		Ctra Comarcal			
		426 Fuengirola/Coin Km15			
	11	Lauro	+34 952 412 767	www.laurogolf.com	3
		Carretera de Malaga a Coin A-404			
		KM14 Alhaurin de la Torre			
		Malaga			
	12	Flamingos	+34 952 889 157	www.flamingos-golf.com	4
		Carretera Cadiz Km 166			
		29600 Marbella			
	13	Santa Clara	+34 952 850 111	www.santaclaragolfmarbella.com	3
		Carretera N-340 Km 187, 500			
		29602 Marbel			
	14	Mijas	+34 952 464 377	www.mijasgolf.org	6
		Urbanizacion Mijas Golf S/N			
		29640 Mijas			
	15	Rio Real	+34 952 765 733	www.rioreal.com	4
		Urbanizacion Golf Rio Real S/N			
		29603 Marbella			
	16	Los Naronjos	+34 952 815 206	www.losnaranjos.com	4
		Urbanizacion Nueva Andalucia S/N			
		29660 Marbella			
	17	Club de Marbella	+34 952 830 500	www.marbellagolf.com	4
		Carretera Cadiz Km 188			
		29600 Marbella			
	18	Parador	+34 952 381 255	www.parador.es/en	5
		Carretera Campo De Golf S/N			
		29004 Malaga			
	19	Atayala	+34 952 882 812	www.atalaya-golf.com	6
		Carretera Benahavis Km 0,700			
		29688 Estepona			

Tenerife					
	20	Tecina Lomada de Tecina 38811 Playa Santiago La Gomera	+34 922 145 950	www.tecinagolf.com	3
	21	Buenavista Club de Golf C/Buenavista del Norte 38480 Santa Cruz de Tenerife	+34 922 129 034	www.buenavistagolf.es	3
	22	Amarilla Golf/Country Club 38639 San Miguel de Abona Santa Cruz de Tenerife	+34 922 730 319	www.amarillagolf.es	4
	23	Golf del Sur 38639 San Miguel de Abona Santa Cruz de Tenerife	+34 922 738 170	www.golfdelsur.net	4
England & Wales					
	24	Brabazon The Belfry Golf Club Wishaw, Sutton Coldfield B76 9PR	08709 00 00 66	www.thebelfry.com	4
	25	PGA National The Belfry Golf Club Wishaw, Sutton Coldfield B76 9PR	08709 00 00 66	www.thebelfry.com	4
	26	Royal St David's Harlech LL46 2UB	01766 780361	www.royalstdavids.co.uk	5
	27	Nefyn & District Golf Club Morfa Nefyn Pwllheli LL53 6DA	01758 720218	www.nefyn-golf-club.com	3
	28	Nailcote Hall Nailcote Lane Berkswell Warwickshire CV7 7DE	02476 466174	www.nailcotehall.co.uk	2
	29	Carden Park Golf Club Chester CH3 9DQ	01829 731000	www.devere.co.uk/deluxe/ carden-park	3
South Africa					
	30	Kimberley Golf Club Transvaal Road Kamjersdam, Kimberley 8301	053 841 0127	www.kimberleygolfclub.co.za	2
	31	Lost City Golf Club Sun City, Pilansberg, NW Province PO Box 5, Sun City 0316	+27 14 557 3902	www.suninternational.com	2
	32	Gary Player Country Club Sun City, NW Province PO Box 6, Sun City 0316	+27 557-1245/6	www.sun-intemational.com	3
	33	Royal Cape Golf Club 174 Ottery Road Wynberg 7800 Western Cape	+27 21 761 6551	www.royalcapegolf.co.za	4
	34	Steenberg Golf Club 10802 Steenberg Estate Tokai Road, Tokai	+27 21 713 2222	www.steenberggolfclub.co.za	4
Florida					
	35	Championsgate The National 400 Masters Blvd Orlando 33837	+01 888 558 9301	www.championsgategolf.com	3

36	Championsgate The Internation 400 Masters Blvd Orlando 33837	+01888 558 9301	www.championsgategolf.com	3
37	Mystic Dunes 7840 Shadow Tree Lane Celebration 34747	+01 787 5678	www.mysticdunesgolf.com	3
38	Celebration 701 Golf Park Drive Celebration 34747	01 407 566-GOLF	www.celebrationgolf.com	4
39	Ridgewood Lakes 200 Eagle Ridge Drive Davenport 33837	+01863 424 8688	www.ridgewoodlakesgolf.com	4
40	Falcons Fire 3200 Seralago Boulevard Kissimmee 34746	+01407 239 5445	www.falconsfire.com	4
41	Highlands Reserve 500 Highlands Reserve Blvd Davenport 33897	+01877 508-4653	www.highlandsreserve-golfcom	4
42	Providence 1518 Clubhouse Blvd Davenport 33837	+01863-420-2652	www.providence-golf.com	4
43	Orange Lakes - The Legend 8505 W Irlo Bronson Memorial Hwy Celebration	+01407 239 0000	www.orangelake.com	4
44	The Club at Eaglebrooke 1300 Eaglebrooke Blvd Lakeland 33813	+01 863-701-0101	www.eaglebrooke.com	3
45	Deer Creek 42749 Highway 27 Davenport	+01863 424-3153	www.deercreekrv.com	5

Australasia

46	Royal Melbourne Cheltenham Road Black Rock VIC 3193	+03 9598 6755	www.royalmelbourne.com.au	1
47	NSW Golf Club Matraville NSW 2036	+02 9661 4455	www.nswgolfc1ub.com.au	1
48	Royal Hobart 79-81 Seven Mile Beach Road Seven Mile Beach TAS 7170	+03 6248 6161	www.rhgc.com.au	4
49	Tasmania Golf Club Country Club Avenue Prospect Vale TAS 7250	+03 6225 7040	www.countryclubtasmania.com.au	3
50	Bambougle Dunes 425 Waterhouse Road Bridport TAS 7262	+03 6356 0094	www.bambougledunes.com.au	2

Asia Hong Kong

51	The Jockey Club Kau Sai Chau Sai Kung Hong Kong	+852 2791-3388	www.kscgolf.com	2

I have often been asked which my favourite holes are and what would constitute the perfect course. I felt unable to just select eighteen different holes so have chosen the best opening hole I have played and so on. Best is not an appropriate choice of word, these holes representing my favourites because they epitomise my philosopy on golf. They must be pretty and pleasing on the eye, enjoyable yet difficult enough to prove a challenge. As you can see, the card proved to be lob-sided at par forty-one out and thirty-four in, but that would be the perfect social golfer's course – a difficult first nine, a few drinks at the turn and a bite to eat, then an easier stroll around the back nine, what could be better.

The Ultimate Social Course

Hole	Course	Par	
1	Alhaurin	5	Just invites a whack and in a perfect location, you just can't wait to get started.
2	Nefyn	5	Superb setting along the cliffs. When last there into the wind, three drivers all well hit and I still couldn't reach the green. Was I bothered, not a jot.
3	Tasmania Golf Club	5	Wonderful location, the drive over the sea offers great rewards but, of course, high risk.
4	Royal Melbourne	5	Truly one of the great holes in golf.
5	New South Wales	5	Never played a finer par five anywhere, the views are sensational.
6	New South Wales	3	Probably the most famous hole in Australia and with good reason.
7	Nailcote Hall	3	Treachorous hole with huge bunker and such a narrow target, easy to hit, hard to stay on.
8	Santa Clara Marbella	5	Superb downhill long hole with views to Africa and Gibraltar
9	Gary Player Country Club	5	Wonderful challenge, to par it is a great feeling.
10	The Brabazon, Belfry	4	You have got to have a crack for the green.
11	Ridgewood Lakes, Orlando	4	Great hole, super drive and approach through two lakes to a narrow bunker protected hole.
12	The Jockey Club, Hong Kong	4	Superb downhill, giving tremendous views of the island's former colony.
13	Lost City Golf Course	3	The crocs … say no more!
14	New South Wales	4	Possibly the most difficult hole in this outstanding course.
15	Barbougle Sands	4	Enthralling, sensational, leaves you wanting more!

16	Championsgate National	4	Short par four heavily protected, dare you go for it!
17	Steenburg	3	Downhill over water, fountains par three, with Table Mountain as backdrop.
18	Carden Park, Cheshire	4	Short par four downhill, stunning views of Snowdonia, high risk/reward hole.

The Social Golfer Medals

	Par 3s	Par 4s	Par 5s
GOLD	New South Wales Hole 6	Royal Melbourne Hole 6	Gary Player C.C. Hole 9
SILVER	Lost City G C Hole 13	New South Wales Hole 14	Santa Clara Hole 8
BRONZE	Nailcote Hall Hole 9	Brabazon Hole 10	New South Wales Hole 5

Accommodation

Hammamet, Tunisia
Magic Life Africa Imperial
BP 48
8057 Yasmine Hammamet
Nabeul
Tunisia
Tel: +216.72.22.70.00. Fax: +216.72.22.61.93
E-mail: unicesu@magiclife.tourism.tn
www.realholidayreports.com/hotel_list/
Magic_Life_Africana_Hammamet.html

Costa del Sol, Spain
El Paraiso
Ctra Cadiz
167 Aptdo
134 Estepona
Marbella 29680
Tel: +34 952 838 556. Fax: +34 952 830 761

Costa del Sol, Spain
Golf Caledonia
Ctra De Cadiz
KM 166
Call Hinojo S.n.urb.be
Estepona
Marbella 29680

Costa del Sol, Spain
Alhaurin Golf
Plaza de la Palmera s/n
29120 Alhaurin el Grande
Malaga
Tel: 952 491 100. Fax: 952 594 375
info@lapalmera.com.es

Gibraltar
Eliott Hotel
Governor's Parade
Gibraltar
Tel: 350 70500. Fax: 350 70243
E-mail: eliott@gibnet.gi
www.gib.gi/eliotthotel

Wales, UK
The Castle Hotel
Castle Square
Harlech
Gwynedd, LL46 2YH
Tel: +44(0)1766 780529
Fax: +44(0)1766 780499
www.harlechcastlehotel.co.uk

West Midlands, UK
The Belfry
Wishaw
Sutton Coldfield
West Midlands
B76 9PR
Tel: +44(0)1675 470301. Fax: +44(0)1675 470256
E-mail: enquirie @the belfry.com
www.thebelfry.co.uk/contact.cfm

Coventry, UK
Nailcote Hall
Nailcote Lane
Berkswell
Warwickshire, CV7 7DE
Tel: +44(0)2476 466174. Fax: +44(0)2476 470720
E-mail: info@nailcotehall.co.uk
www.nailcotehall.co.uk

Hong Kong, China
Harbour Plaza Hong Kong
20 Tak Fung Street
Whampoa Garden
Hunghom
Kowloon
Hong Kong
Tel: (852) 2996 8006. Fax: (852) 2621 3318
E-mail: rsvn.hphk@harbour-plaza.com
www.harbour-plaza.com/hphk

South Africa
The Table Bay Hotel
Quay Six
V & A Waterfront
Cape Town
Contact: Ryan Mackie
Tel: +27 (0)21 794 9050. Fax: +27 (0)21 794 9995
Mobile: +27 (0)82 782 3141
www.sa-venues.com/visit/thetablebayhotel

South Africa
Flamingo Casino
N12 Transvaal Road
PO Box 668
Kimberley 8301
Tel: +27 53 830 2600. Fax: +27 53 830 2601
E-mail: flamingo@sunint.co.za
www.suninternational.com/destinations/
casinos/flamingo

Florida, USA
Orlando Resort
417 Lakeshore Parkway
Davenport
Florida 33896

Tenerife
Golf del Sur Villa
Tenerife
Contact: John Roberts (Senior)
Tel: 01925 730924
www.holiday-rentals.co.uk/
golf-del sur/s/1965/fa/find.squery

Cheshire, UK
Carden Park Hotel
Nr Chester
Cheshire , CH3 9DQ
Tel: 01829/731000. Fax: 01829 731032
www.devere.co.uk/deluxe/carden-park

Australia
Wrest Point Casino
410 Sandy Bay Road
Sandy Bay
Tasmanai 7005
Tel: 1800 703 006
E-mail: email@wrestpoint.com.au
www.wrestpoint.com.au

Australia
Saville on Russell
222 Russell Street
Melbourne
VIC 3000
Tel: +61 3 9915 2500 or 2507 (direct). Fax: +61 3 9915 2598
E-mail: russell.info@savillehotelgroup.com
www.savillehotelgroup.com

Australia
Shangri-La Hotel
176 Cumberland Street
The Rocks
Sydney
NSW 2000
Tel: +61 2 9250 6000. Fax: +61 2 9250 6250
www.shangri-la.com/en/property/sydney/shangrila

14. Conclusion

My aim in writing this journal was principally to show future stroke sufferers that with the support of family, friends and the outstanding professionals in the NHS and at the Stroke Association, there is still a fulfilling lifestyle still available. When I had my stroke and felt totally unzipped from my left hand side, thankfully there were professionals in the Health Service who could help to reunite the parts of the body lost to your brain. Like a proper zip, the new one can never feel exactly the same but it works and fulfils its function anyway. With luck, all stroke sufferers can get back to some normality and even use the weaknesses as positives. With golf, my swing is now much more secure without the rotating hips of my left side. My lost weight has helped my athleticism. The stroke was a bit of a drastic way to move on, but it has happened, I have to deal with it and carry on the good work of both hospital units.

As a thank you for the support I was given , I now dedicate a proportion of my life to charitable work on behalf of the Stroke Association and in particular, our Stroke Awareness Campaign. By reading this book, you are contributing to this campaign. Thank you.

Golf is such a big part of my life and has been the catalyst for much of my recovery. That my wife is now showing an interest has given me great joy. The social golf trips are so enjoyable to plan. During the next two years, there are plans to visit Dubai and the Barnato in Kimberley. In 2010, I plan a re-attack on Tasmania and to visit North Island in New Zealand, especially Cape Kidnappers and Kauri Cliffs. We also fancy re-visiting Vegas and California, so I have great expectations that this will not be the only volume. Watch this space!

Since my stroke, my golf game has not worsened at all. Indeed, because of my tablets, I presume, I no longer fret over four footers, I simply hit and if it goes in, that's great, if not, so what. I no longer need to use my best wood, my pencil to write my score down – it's irrelevant. I now play golf the way the elders intended it to be played. As Kenny used to say, you start at A and end up at B and play wherever it rests in the meantime, with no drops, no preferred lies. Seven is not a dirty number, taking seven is better than not playing at all. I love playing and being in the company of good players – you cannot fail to admire their skill and technique. Mulligans are a thing of the past, every shot is important; you never know, it could be your last, so enjoy it.

Golf is very similar to life, from the day we are born, we make choices that affect the route, quality and length of our life. It's like standing on the first tee. Accomplished players practise, do not commence the round without thoroughly going through a well-structured, pre-round routine and then they follow a regimented approach to each shot on the course. This is what sets them apart from the social golfer. No pre- match pints, just putts. Every professional I have met has stressed that this is the main difference between them and us – they work at it, respect and know the course and its difficulties, and put themselves in the best possible condition to play and score well. As a social golfer, my approach to a round of golf now is diametrically opposite, in that enjoyment and fulfillment are complete antipodes from the reward, success and result-orientated readiness of the true practitioner. What I can say however is that I have tried to bring the pro golfers' mentality and complete trust in their preparation into my daily battle to pursue a long and healthy lifestyle. The discipline that Tiger shows in his golfing success can be transmitted to a stroke victim's battle to reduce the chances of another attack.

I cannot help but wonder whether, like my father, I will have a further but fatal attack some time in the future. However like the approach over water, I have to try to ensure this does not come into my daily mindset. Tiger knows how far he can hit the ball and trusts his swing. I am eating better, my weight is down, my blood pressure is regularly tested; my preparation could not be better, so there is no reason why I should not lead a full life. Tiger knows good things will happen on the golf course, I now try to ensure that good things will happen in my life. His course management is supreme, my lifestyle management has to be equally so. He implicity trusts his caddy, Steve Williams, I now have to have equal faith in those around me. Tiger is simply so focused on every shot, and I try to focus deeply on each moment and squeeze all the positive feelings from each and every opportunity that arises. He rarely makes the same mistake twice. I try not to. If something makes me tired, I do not do it again. You can't win at golf and cheat, the rules, draconian though they are, ensure that it cannot happen. Life is like that, your body is your temple, listen to it at all times, it never lies. There are no short-cuts. Prepare well and you score well. Live healthily and you may live longer, it's the same principle.

Winners are grinners, every golf champion smiles. I love smiling, there is nothing better than being happy. I have now concluded the book and I am smiling now. I hope some of you feel the need to visit those places I have attempted to adequately describe in this text. More importantly, I hope for those of you who are sufferers like me, you may take some positives out of my small achievements since my stroke.

> **To all golfers, enjoy each and every round** – play with honesty and integrity, and treat each shot as special, like every moment in a day. Sadly, one day for all of us, we will have played our last shot, so always ensure you enjoyed that last round you played.

> **Monitor your blood pressure regularly** – high blood pressure can ruin your game and your life, no matter what your age.

15. Stroke — Act Fast information

If you suspect that someone is having a stroke **ACT FAST**

With over 150,000 people inthe UK having a stroke every year, it is imperative that people can recognise a stroke when it's happening and take prompt action.

What is FAST?

FAST requires an assessment of three specific symptoms of stroke:

Facial weakness – can the person smile? Has their mouth or eye drooped?
Arm weakness – can the person raise both arms?
Speech problems – can the person speak clearly and understand what you say?
Test all three symptoms.

If the person has failed any one of these tests, you must call 999. Stroke is a medical emergency and by calling 999 you can help someone reach hospital quickly and receive the early treatment they need.

Steps to reduce your risk
There are some steps that you and your doctor can take together.
Get your blood pressure checked.
High blood pressure causes the arteries to fur up (atherosclerosis) and puts extra strain on the blood vessels. You may not know if you have high blood pressure, so you should have it checked regularly. (A normal healthy adult blood pressure is less than 140/90mmHg)
Make sure other medical conditions are controlled.

A number of other medical problems increase your risk of a stroke including:

Heart disease
Atrial fibrillation (irregular heartbeat)
High cholesterol
Diabetes